Around the Year in Japan

装　幀 ● 菊地　信義

装　画 ● 野村　俊夫

本文レイアウト ● 山下　恭弘

イラスト ● 山井　教雄

編集協力 ● 清水　宏充

- 本書は、NHKで放送された日本語と英語のそれぞれ別の台本をベースとしています。そのため、対訳になっていない部分があります。また、編集部の判断で用語や表記の統一などを行いました。
- 項目の最後にある語句解説は、講談社刊行『日本語大辞典(第二版)』より引用したものです。
- 覚えておきたい表現や難しい単語は、太字で和文と英文を対照させてありますので、ご利用下さい。

Published by Kodansha International Ltd.,
17-14, Otowa 1-chome, Bunkyo-ku, Tokyo 112–8652.

First Edition 1998

ISBN4-7700-2457-6
98 99 00 10 9 8 7 6 5 4 3 2 1

NHK「日本ひとくち歳時記」
Around the Year in Japan

NHK国際放送局
「日本一口事典」プロジェクト［編］

まえがき

　日本には、春夏秋冬の季節ごとに暮らしに密着した独特の文化があります。豊かな四季に恵まれた風土のなかで、長年にわたって培われた慣習や日本人のものの考え方は、他国にはないユニークなものが少なくありません。

　NHKの国際放送「NHKワールド・ラジオ日本」では、このような日本独自の文化、伝統を外国の方にも理解していただこうと、毎回一つのキーワードを選び、「日本一口事典」として、世界に向け放送しています。

　本書は、この番組で放送したもののなかからとりわけ好評だったものを季節ごとに再構成し、『日本ひとくち歳時記』としてまとめたものです。

　日本人は、遠く遣唐使の昔から、近くは明治以来の西洋文明導入にいたるまで、外国の先進文化を取り入れることに長けてきました。

　しかし、自分たち日本のことを説明すること、すなわち自らを発信することは、国際化が進展したといわれるいまでも、依然として不得意としています。

　それは、日本人が「はにかみや」だったというよりも、"ツール"としての適切な言葉、言い回しを知らなかった、あるいは知ろうとしなかったことに、大きな原因があるのではないでしょうか。それを克服する

Preface

Japanese culture has been deeply influenced by the fact that the people had to live in accordance with the changes that occur in each of four different seasons. As a result, there are many things about the customs and ways of thinking in Japan, fostered over hundreds of years in a national environment blessed by a rich variety, that are unique and not seen in other countries.

It was with a view to telling people from other countries about these peculiar traditions and cultures in Japan that NHK's International Broadcasting Division broadcast a weekly program named "Japan Memo," with each program centering on explanation of one particular word.

In this book we have taken words that received a particularly favorable response from our listeners, and rearranged them in the order of the four seasons, under the new title of *Around the Year in Japan*.

The Japanese have always been adept at adopting advanced cultures from foreign countries: in ancient times, it was from the messengers of T'ang China, and in the more recent past, from the Meiji period onwards, it was from the civilization of the West.

When it comes to explaining their own country, that is to say, communicating about themselves, however, Japanese have remind as inept as ever—even today, in the age of so-called Internationalization.

The reason for this is not so much that Japanese are particularly bashful, but rather that they have been unaware of the appropriate words and expressions to use as "tools," or perhaps they have not made enough effort to get to know them. To remedy this situation, surely an indispensable first

には、何よりも私たち日本人が日本文化についてよく理解することが、不可欠と言えるでしょう。

　実際、外国の方と交流の場で「日本人にとってあたりまえの習慣を、外国人にどう伝えたらいいのか?」「日本語で使い慣れた単語を英語ではどう表現するのか?」こんな悩みをもたれる方は少なくないようです。

　本書はこうした声にこたえるべく、一冊にまとめたものです。この本を読み進めていただければ、"知っていると思っていた日本のことがらも、あらためて問われると案外理解していなかった""日本語で使い慣れた表現は英語ではこんな言い方をするのか"などと、数々の「新鮮な発見」があるものと自負しています。

　インターネットで世界中の人たちと自由にコミュニケーションできるいま、英語は世界の共通語になりつつあります。英語を媒介とすれば、欧米だけでなく、世界中の人たちと意見を交換し、理解しあうことが可能となります。

　本書をお読みいただいたみなさんが、それぞれの身近なところから日本文化の伝え手となり、草の根の交流を国際的に拡げて行く。そのような活動にこの本がお役に立てるならば、これにまさる喜びはありません。

NHK国際放送局

松澤　幹治

step is to gain a thorough understanding of the culture of our own country.

In dealings with people from other countries, it seems that many Japanese find themselves coming up against certain common problems. A particular custom might seem obvious to Japanese, but how best to explain it to someone from a foreign country? A particular word might be commonplace in Japanese, but how to express it in English?

This book was put together with the aim of answering such difficulties. We also firmly believe that it will be delight-fully informative in countless other ways: our readers may well discover aspects of Japan they didn't know about before, or understood imperfectly. They will discover that there are indeed ways of expressing various Japanese phrases in English.

In an age when the Internet is enabling people all over the world to communicate freely with each other, English is becom-ing more and more indispensable as a common international language. Using the medium of English, it becomes possible to communicate and exchange opinions not only with the countries of Europe and America, but all over the world.

Reading this book will enable each reader to become an ambassador at the personal level, able to explain Japanese culture to people all around the world. It would give us the greatest joy and satisfaction if our book could be of help in any activity of this kind.

Matsuzawa Kanji
International Planning & Broadcasting Department, NHK

目　次

CONTENTS

第3章 秋

第4章 冬

Part 3 Autumn

Part 4 Winter

春 Spring

Part 1

ひな祭り
Doll Festival

日本ひとくち歳時記、今日は「ひな祭り」について
お話ししましょう。

*This is Around the Year in Japan. Today we are
going to talk about Hina Matsuri, or the "Doll
Festival."*

**ひな人形の飾り方の
決まりごとは?**

日本では3月3日はひな祭りといって、女の子の成長を祝う日です。別名、桃の節句ともいいます。この日、女の子のいる家では、ひな人形と呼ばれる人形を飾って**ごちそう**を食べ、楽しいひとときを過ごします。

もっとも標準的なひな飾りをご紹介しましょう。

階段状にしつらえた飾り棚に赤いもうせんを敷き、その上に15体の人形を並べていくのです。これは昔の貴族の生活をかたどったものです。

まず一番上の段には**金屏風**を立て、その前に**天皇**と**皇后**になぞらえた男女一対の人形を置きます。2段目には宮廷に仕える3人の女性たち、3段目には、笛や太鼓を手にした5人のお

In Japan, March 3 is a special festival day called *Hina Matsuri*, or the Doll Festival, meant to celebrate young girls' growth and development. Another name for this day is the Peach Festival. Any families with little girls will put up a display of special little dolls known as *hina ningyō*, and there will also be a celebration with some **special treats** to eat.

The following is the standard way Japanese people celebrate the festival.

The little dolls are usually displayed in a particular way. They usually stand in several tiers on a special stepped unit, known as the *hina-dan*, laid with bright red cloth. Fifteen different dolls, all brilliantly costumed, go on these tiers.

On the topmost level stands a **gilt** folding screen in the ancient court style, and in front of that are placed two dolls who represent the ancient **Emperor** and **Empress**. On the second level are three court ladies in waiting, and on the third, five musicians performing on flute, drums and other

囃子。4段目には2人の**大臣**。5段目
に家具のミニチュア類。6段目には3
人の護衛の者たち。7段目に、**かご**
(乗り物)や牛車を並べます。

このほか欠かせないのが、桃の木と
橘 の木、中に灯をともす一対のぼん
ぼり、菱形をした赤、白、緑の3色の
餅を重ねた菱餅などがあります。

このひな祭りの歴史をたどると、今
から**1000年**以上も前、**貴族**の少女た
ちが紙で作った一対の男女の人形を
用いて遊んだ「ままごと遊び」にまで
さかのぼります。この人形を「ひいな」
と呼びましたが、これは当時の言葉で
「小さくてかわいい」という意味です。

また、この「ひいな遊び」とは別
に、季節の変わり目に神々に飲食を
供えて無病息災を祈る信仰があり、
こうした日を「節句」と呼んでいま
した。3月の節句では、紙で作った人
形で体をなでて汚れを払い、その人
形を水に流す行事が行われ、これと
「ひいな遊び」とが混ざりあってしだ
いに今日の「ひな祭り」が形作られ
ていったのです。

**貴族の遊びから
始まったひな祭り**

instruments. On the fourth level are two **state ministers** (minister of the left and minister of the right). On the fifth are exquisite miniature replicas of furniture and other goods used by the aristocracy in ancient Japan. On the sixth level are three guards, and on the seventh, such items as a **palanquin** and an ox-cart.

Other items indispensable to the display are peach and mandarin orange trees, a pair of white paper lanterns with some kind of lighting inside, and special diamond-shaped rice cakes in red, white and green.

The history of the Doll Festival stretches back over a **millennium** to the time when daughters of the **aristocracy** used to play house with men and women dolls made out of paper. These dolls were referred to as *hiina*, a word which in those days meant "small and cute."

Quite apart from these games with *hiina* dolls, dolls were also used in festivals in the religious life of the people. People made offerings to the gods and prayed for good health at certain times of the year, such as the change of seasons. There was a particular festival in March in which the participants rubbed their bodies with paper dolls to remove pollution, and then cast the dolls into the river or sea and allowed them to float away, taking the pollution with them. This tradition then blended with the children's games with paper dolls, and even-

　今日のような階段状の飾りが普及したのは17世紀の末ごろからで、また、このころからひな祭りが女の子の祭りとして定着し、女の子が生まれて最初にめぐってきた3月3日にひな飾りを贈る風習もできました。飾りも2段、3段から7段、8段と、次第に豪華なものとなり、あまりに**華美である**というので、時の政府が製作を**禁じた**こともしばしばあったほどでした。

住宅スペースに左右されるひな飾り

　今日、もっとも典型的なひな飾りは先ほど述べたように7段程度で、高さは大人の背の高さ近くになりますが、最近は住宅事情が悪く、このようなひな飾りを飾るスペースがないという家も少なくありません。

　そこで、男女一対の簡素なひな人形がよく売れているということですが、やはり段飾りの豪華さとは比べ物になりません。毎年1度、人形を箱から出して段に並べる楽しさは、女の子にとって格別のもので、少女時代の**懐かしい思い出**になるようです。

　日本ひとくち歳時記、今日は「ひな祭り」についてお話ししました。

tually became the *Hina Matsuri* as it is celebrated today.

The displays of dolls we see today became popular from the end of the 17th century. It was around this time that the *Hina Matsuri* became celebrated as a festival particularly for girls, and the custom arose of celebrating the doll festival on the first March 3 after a girl's birth. At first the displays consisted of just two or three levels, but they soon grew to seven or eight, eventually becoming so **ornate** that periodically the government **banned** their manufacture.

Today the typical doll display is, as we said earlier, seven tiers or less in height, but nearly as tall as the average adult. In recent years, however, conditions in houses have not been conducive to such large displays, as many homes lack sufficient space.

Scaled-down displays of male and female dolls in pairs are apparently popular, even though they cannot match the splendor of the traditional doll sets. The pleasure of taking the dolls out of their boxes once a year and placing them on the stand is a ritual that little girls enjoy, and one all women recall with special **nostalgia**.

This has been *Around the Year in Japan*. On today's program we discussed *Hina Matsuri*, or the "Doll Festival."

卒業式
Commencement Exercises

日本ひとくち歳時記、今日は「卒業式」について
お話ししましょう。

This is Around the Year in Japan. Today we are
going to talk about *sotsugyōshiki*, or
"commencement exercises."

**3月は日本中で
卒業式が行われる**

日本では小学校から大学まで、すべての教育機関の新学年が4月に始まります。したがって卒業はその前の月、3月になります。それぞれの学校への入学、卒業は人生の大切な節目と考えられ、3月の中旬から下旬にかけて、小、中、高校や大学、**専門学校**で卒業式が行われます。

場所はたいていその学校の**講堂**か**体育館**です。規模の大きな大学などの場合、どこか大きなホールなどを借り切って卒業式をするところもあります。

特に決まりがあるわけではありませんが、小学校から高校まで、式次第はほぼ一定です。式場の前中央に卒業生の席が用意され、その周りに在校生や父母が席を占めます。

In Japan, the academic year begins in April—for all educational institutions, from elementary school to university—so graduation occurs in March. Ceremonies for both admission and graduation from each of the various levels are considered an important milestone in life. From mid to late March, elementary, junior high and high schools, as well as universities and specialized **professional schools**, hold commencement exercises.

For the most part the school **auditorium** or **gymnasium** is where the ceremony takes place, but larger institutions such as universities may sometimes reserve huge public halls or other places in order to accommodate the participants and guests.

In general, the same procedural forms for the commencement exercises are followed by elementary, middle and high schools, although no hard and fast rules exist. The graduating students all have seats situated in the central area of the ceremonial hall, towards the front,

卒業式の式次第はどうなっている？

　まず、卒業生がクラス担任の教師に先導されて入場します。**教頭**が卒業式の開始を宣言し、**校歌**が歌われます。卒業生の名前が呼ばれ、壇上に用意された**卒業証書**を校長から受け取ります。

　たいてい全員が順番に壇上に上がって受け取りますが、卒業生を代表する生徒に渡される時もあります。卒業式は卒業証書を授与するためのセレモニーですから、この部分が式のハイライトということになります。

　その後、校長先生や父母の代表であるPTA会長、その他の来賓の**祝辞**が続きます。別れや旅立ちの歌が歌われ、在校生代表の卒業生を送る言葉「**送辞**」、それに答える**卒業生代表**の「答辞」で式は締めくくられます。

　式の後、卒業生はそれぞれのクラスに分かれて担任の先生やクラスメートと別れの挨拶をします。在校中

and around them sit the students still attending the school and the parents.

The commencement exercise starts with a procession of graduating students into the auditorium led by the class teachers. The **vice principal** announces the formal start of the ceremony, and the **school anthem** is sung. Then the names of the graduating students are read off one by one, and each goes up to the principal at the podium to receive his or her **diploma**.

Usually, everybody goes up in turn as the names are called, but sometimes a single representative student receives the diplomas. The graduation ceremony centers on this giving out of the diplomas, so this is the highlight of the entire ceremony.

After that, there are **words of congratulations** from the principal and the chairperson of the Parents and Teachers Association, who represents the parents, as well as specially invited guests. Then the students sing farewell songs and songs that mark new departures in life, and there is a **farewell address** given by a representative of the students continuing on at the school. The ceremony winds up with a reply on behalf of the graduating students from the **class valedictorian**.

With the ceremony over, graduating students in the same class get together to say goodbye to each other and to their teachers. **Commemorative albums** are given out,

の学校行事などの折に写した思い出の写真や、卒業に当たって将来の進路や夢などを書き綴った作文などを載せた**記念のアルバム**が配られます。先生や在校生に見送られ、卒業生は花束と卒業証書の入った筒、そして卒業アルバムを手に、これまで通い続けた**母校**を後にします。

卒業式の後、在学中にお世話になった先生や学校職員などに感謝する**謝恩会**が催されます。

気楽な雰囲気で行われる謝恩会

学校がそのまま謝恩会の会場になる場合もありますし、場所を移してどこか会食のできる所で行う場合もあります。大学の場合にはホテルの宴会場を借りて開くことが多いようです。

卒業式は終始、緊張した**厳粛な雰囲気**の中で行われることが多く、挨拶や祝辞もどちらかといえば上級の学校へ進んだり、社会へ出てゆく学生、生徒たちへの励ましや戒めの言葉になります。肩の凝らない雰囲気の中での謝恩会や、その後の2次会が友人同士が心おきなく別れを惜しむ場になります。

with photos of school events students have participated in, and essays describing their plans and dreams for the future and so on. The graduating students then leave their **alma mater**, the school they have attended for several years, with bouquets of flowers, their diplomas in cardboard tubes, and commemorative albums, seen off by teachers and continuing students.

After the commencement exercise, there is usually a **thank-you party** to express appreciation to the teachers and school staff who looked after the students while they were still in school.

Sometimes this party takes place at the school itself, but often it is held in a facility off-campus where food can be served. If it is a university graduation, in many cases a banquet hall at a hotel will be rented for the occasion.

Generally the commencement exercises are carried out in a highly charged, **solemn atmosphere**, and the addresses and congratulatory speeches consist of words of advice to study hard if the students are going on to a higher level of education, or various kinds of counsel if they are heading out into the working world. At the thank-you parties and smaller gatherings that follow, the students get the chance to bid each other farewell in a more relaxed, heartwarming atmosphere.

　1998年に卒業を迎える小、中、高校生は合わせて438万人余りです。卒業式が終わるとそれぞれの学校で、新入生を迎える準備が始まります。そして4月初旬の**入学式**を迎えるのです。

　日本ひとくち歳時記、今日は「卒業式」についてお話ししました。

In 1998, 4.38 million youngsters graduated from elementary, junior high and high schools in Japan. Once the commencement exercises are over, the schools immediately begin preparations for welcoming new students. The **matriculation ceremony** for new students is held at the beginning of April.

This has been *Around the Year in Japan*. On today's program we discussed *sotsugyōshiki*, or "commencement exercises."

花　見
Cherry Blossom Viewing

日本ひとくち歳時記、今日は「花見」について
お話ししましょう

This is *Around the Year in Japan*. Today we are
going to talk about *hanami*, or "Cherry Blossom
Viewing."

**桜は日本人が
もっとも好む花**

日本の4月を象徴するものといったら、何といっても桜でしょう。桜ほど日本人に親しまれている花はないといっても過言ではありません。

桜の花は白からピンクの間のさまざまな色合いで、一つ一つの花は**直径2〜3センチ**と小さなものですが、これが木いっぱいに咲き誇ると、淡いピンクの綿雲が浮かんでいるようで、いかにも春らしいのどかさを感じさせます。

桜には多くの種類があり、自然品種だけで30種以上、これらを**つぎ木**などで品種改良した栽培品種が百余種もあります。

なかでももっともポピュラーなのが「ソメイヨシノ」という品種で、このソメイヨシノの開花日を一般に桜の開花日としています。「今日、東京で桜が

Every April means one thing in particular to the Japanese: the arrival of the cherry blossoms. It is no exaggeration to say that the *sakura*, or cherry, is the flower closest to people's heart.

The color of the cherry blossom can be anything from pure white to deep pink. Though each flower measures a mere two to three centimeters in **diameter**, when an entire tree is covered with the blossoms it appears to float in a beautiful pale pink haze, the very picture of warm, gentle spring.

There are numerous varieties of cherry—more than thirty natural varieties alone, and over a hundred that have been artificially improved through **grafting**.

The most famous variety is the *Somei Yoshino*, and when news reporters announce that the cherry trees have come into bloom, it is this variety they are referring to.

開花しました」というときは、このソメイヨシノが開花したということです。

さて、日本人が桜というと、まず思い浮かべるのが「花見」ではないでしょうか。

桜の花がほころびだすと、公園や川の堤防、神社や寺の境内など、桜がまとまって生えている場所に人々が繰り出して、敷物を敷いて座り、お酒を飲みご馳走を食べて、歌を歌ったりしている姿が目につきます。家族や友人同士、また**職場の同僚**などのグループが、時には夜遅くまで、桜見物に事寄せて、賑やかなひとときを過ごすのです。

ところで、この「花見」という行事、元来は農業に関係した儀礼だったといわれています。稲作業が始まる前、**旧暦**の3月3日から4月8日までの間に、山から花を手折って来て**軒先**に吊るすとか、あるいは、屋外に**カマド**を設けて共同飲食をする、などしたのが、もともとの姿だったようです。

行楽としての「花見」は、9世紀ごろにはすでに**貴族**の遊びとして行われており、それが武家に受け継がれ

元々は農業の儀礼として始まった花見

With the mention of cherry blossoms, the first thing that comes to most Japanese people's mind is probably *hanami*, or flower viewing.

As soon as the cherry blossoms start to show, people flock to parks, riversides, shrines, temples—wherever a good number of the trees can be found—spread out mats to sit on, and enjoy themselves drinking *sake* and singing popular songs. Groups of family members, friends or **working colleagues** gather to enjoy the sight of the blossoms, and sometimes the fun lasts deep into the night.

This custom of flower viewing apparently started as a religious festival associated with agriculture, originally held between March 3 and April 8 by the **old lunar calendar**, before farm work started for the year; apparently people brought branches of cherry blossoms down from the trees on the mountainsides and hung them from the **eaves** of their houses in the village, and there were other celebrations like a communal feast around an open **hearth** outside.

Hanami as a form of entertainment seems to have already taken root among **aristocrats** in the 9th century. The *samurai* warrior class later adopted it, and by the start

て、17世紀に始まる江戸時代になると庶民の娯楽へと広がっていきました。そのころには、山野に自然に生える桜を愛でるだけでなく、河岸や神社、寺の境内などに人工的に桜を植えて楽しむようになりました。

働き蜂の日本人も花見だけは例外

こうした場所は、今も桜の名所として多くの花見客を集めています。特に人出の多い所には、軽食を売る出店が出て、日が暮れると、そうした店の明かりに照らされた桜が夜空に白く浮き出して独特の雰囲気を醸し出します。

この桜の季節、夜風はまだ冷たいのですが、夜の宴のために朝から場所を取る人も出るほど。普段は「**働き蜂**」といわれるほど、仕事第一の日本人の行楽好きの一面を覗かせる行事だといえるでしょう。

日本ひとくち歳時記、今日は「花見」についてお話ししました。

of the Edo period (1600–1868), it had become a pastime enjoyed by ordinary folk too. It was in this period that flowering cherry trees started to be planted on the grounds of shrines and temples, and on riverbanks and other places so they could be enjoyed there, rather than simply being left to grow in the mountains and fields.

Some of these places have now become particularly renowned for their cherry blossoms, and they attract countless people eager to see their flowers. At the most popular, food stalls are set up with light refreshments, and as dusk falls, the light from these stalls makes the cherry blossoms seem to loom white against the night sky, producing a particularly special atmosphere.

The night breezes at this time of year can still be slightly chilly, but nevertheless nighttime viewing is so popular that some people arrive in the morning to stake out places under the trees, which they reserve all day for a party in the evening. The practice reveals another, pleasure-loving side to the Japanese, usually far more famous as **worker bees** who put work before anything else.

This has been *Around the Year in Japan*. On today's program we discussed *hanami*, or "Cherry Blossom Viewing."

こいのぼり
Carp Streamers

日本ひとくち歳時記、今日は「こいのぼり」について
お話ししましょう。

This is *Around the Year in Japan*. Today we are
going to talk about *koi-nobori*, or "carp streamers."

**こいのぼりは
子供の日のシンボル**

4月も半ばを過ぎると日本の空に
は数メートルにもなる大きな魚
が泳ぎ始めます。もちろん、本物の
魚ではありません。棒の先に吊るさ
れた布製の魚で「こいのぼり」といい、
5月5日の**子供の日**のために飾られる
ものです。

5月5日は、もともとは「端午の節
句」と呼ばれ、災厄や病気を払う厄
払いの**行事**が行われる日でした。

8世紀ごろの記録には、**ショウブ**や
ヨモギなど、香りの強い植物を身に
着けたり**軒**にさして魔よけとしたと記
されています。

この「ショウブ」という植物の名
前が、日本語では『武事を重んじる』
という言葉と同じ音であることから、

From around mid-April, you often see great big fish several meters long swimming in the Japanese skies. Not real fish of course. These are *koi-nobori*, or fish made out of cloth and attached like pennants to the tops of poles. They are the decorations used to celebrate May 5, which in Japan is **Children's Day**.

May 5, originally a day in the annual calendar when **rites** were carried out to keep away misfortune and illness, was known as the *Tango* Festival.

Accounts from the 8th century tell how people would attach Japanese irises or **sweetflag** (*shōbu*), **mugwort** and other strongly scented plants to their clothes and to the **eaves** of their houses in an effort to keep evil influences at bay.

It is thought that because of the association of the *bu* in *shōbu* with the *bu* in *buji o omonjiru* (a phrase meaning to put a high value on martial prowess or victory),

次第に男の子の成長を祝う日に転化したのだといわれています。

江戸時代の初め、つまり17世紀ごろには、武士の家ではこの日に**家の紋**を付けた旗などを門口に立てることが流行し、これに対抗して町人たちがこいのぼりを立てるようになったのだといわれています。

こいのぼりは町人の対抗意識の産物

では、なぜ魚の中でも鯉（こい）が選ばれたのでしょうか。

これは中国の古い言い伝えが元になっています。それによれば、黄河の中流に流れの激しい所があり、ここを泳ぎ上った鯉は竜になるとされていることから、鯉が立身出世の象徴として用いられるようになったのです。

都会では小ぶりのこいのぼりが人気

さて、このこいのぼり、もともとは紙で作られていましたが、現在は布で作るのが大部分で、特にナイロン製が大半を占めています。

大手こいのぼりメーカーによると孫の誕生日のお祝いに祖父母が買って贈り物にする場合が多く、**都会**では、最近の住宅事情を反映して、アパートのベランダに飾る、魚の長さ1.5メートルほどのものがよく売れているそうです。

this day came to be celebrated for the healthy growth of boys to manhood.

Some time around the start of the Edo period (1600–1868), *samurai* families started to fly pennants with their **family crests** in front of their homes or living quarters. The story goes that merchants and townsfolk began to fly paper streamers representing carp in an effort to assert their own identity.

Why did they choose **carp** in particular?

The reason derives from an ancient Chinese legend which tells of extremely turbulent rapids in the middle reaches of the Yangtze River, where the carp swimming upstream were apparently transformed into dragons. The carp thus became a symbol of success in life and making one's mark in the world.

Carp streamers were originally made of paper, but nowadays for the most part they are made of cloth, usually nylon.

Major manufacturers claim that in a lot of cases grandparents purchase carp streamers as gifts to celebrate the birth of a grandchild. In **urban areas**, it is quite common to see them flying from the verandas of apartment houses—indicative of the most common form of abode for people nowadays—and *koi-nobori* about 1.5 meters long are said to sell especially well.

**こいのぼりは
3〜6万円の品が人気**

　黒いおとうさん鯉、赤いおかあさん鯉、青い子供の鯉、そして、棒の先に付ける**風車**と、鯉を棒につなぐロールがセットになって3万円から6万円のものが人気だということですが、**広い庭**のある家では、5メートル以上あるこいのぼりが、屋根の上高**くはためいている**姿が見受けられます。

　日本ひとくち歳時記、今日は「こいのぼり」についてお話ししました。

Sets of the pennants, consisting of a black "father" carp, a red "mother" carp, and blue "children" carp, together with a small decorative **windmill** to attach to the top of the pole, and ropes and pulleys with which to string the carp up, are said to be popular, selling from anything between 30,000 and 60,000 yen. If a family has an especially **spacious garden**, you might see a huge carp more than five meters long **fluttering** high above the rooftops.

This has been *Around the Year in Japan*. On today's program we discussed *koi-nobóri*, or "carp streamers."

鯉幟 こいのぼり
紙または布でコイをかたどった吹き流し形の幟。端午の節句に戸外へ立てる縁起物。立身出世のたとえであるコイの滝のぼりを象徴。五月幟 (さつきのぼり)。幟。

花粉症
Hay Fever

日本ひとくち歳時記、今日は「花粉症」について
お話ししましょう。

This is *Around the Year in Japan*. Today we are
going to talk about *kafunshō*, or "hay fever."

**花粉症は2、3月から
秋まで続く**

春先になるとよく、くしゃみや鼻水に悩まされ、目を真っ赤にして、大きなマスクやサングラスをしている人を見かけます。多くの場合、風邪をひいているのではなく「花粉症」という、特定の花粉のせいで起きる鼻のアレルギーのためなのです。

特に杉花粉のアレルギーに苦しむ人が多く、杉の花の咲き始める2月から3月にかけて、**日本列島**の南から北へと「花粉症」の**症状**を訴える人が増えていきます。症状が**花粉**の飛ぶ春先だけでなく、夏から秋まで続く人もいます。

ただし、沖縄と北海道には**杉の木**がないので、「花粉症」はないといわれています。

日本で、「花粉症」という言葉が一

ハークション！

With the arrival of spring, many people in Japan can be seen **sneezing** and **sniffling**, their eyes **bloodshot** behind sunglasses, and large cotton masks over their mouth and nose. They are not suffering from colds, but rather from *kafunshō*, or hay fever, the allergy to pollen—especially pollen from crypotemeria trees.

In February and March in Japan these trees come into flower, and from one end of the **Japanese archipelego** to the other, as the effects of the season spread up the islands, more and more people begin to develop typical hay fever **symptoms**. For some people the symptoms stay on well beyond spring when the **pollen** is actually in the air, into the summer and autumn.

Okinawa and Hokkaidō are the only places that escape hay fever. Apparently, no **cryptomeria trees** are to be found there, and hay fever is said not to exist at all.

In Japan the term "hay fever" only came into gen-

般的に使われるようになったのは、患者数が急激に増えたここ十数年のことです。最近では患者の年齢層も広がり、都市部では人口のおよそ10パーセントが「花粉症」であるともいわれています。

では、どうして近年、急に患者が増えたのでしょうか。

一つには、第2次世界大戦後に大量に植林された杉の木が生長し、花をつけるようになったことがあげられます。

さらに、自動車の**排気ガス**などによる**大気汚染**や、都市生活のストレスも何らかの影響を及ぼしていると考えられています。アスファルト舗装のせいで、花粉がいつまでも地面に吸収されず、何度も舞い上がることも指摘されています。

ところで、**日本気象協会**は、「花粉症」に苦しむ人の増加に伴い、10年前から、天気予報の中で「杉花粉情報」を流すようになりました。

杉の花粉は天気が良く、暖かい南西の風が吹く日に多く飛びます。湿度の高い雨の日には比較的少なくなります。

花粉症患者が急激に増えた理由は?

eral use a decade or so ago, and since then the number of sufferers has increased dramatically. The condition has also started to affect a wider age range: in some urban areas as much as 10 percent of the residents reportedly suffer from hay fever.

But why should it be in the last few years that the number of allergy sufferers has risen so steeply?

One reason may be that it is only recently that the numerous cryptomeria trees planted after World War II have grown to maturity and are producing cones.

Other factors may be the effects of **air pollution** caused by **gas emissions** from motor vehicles, and the stress caused by the daily grind of life in the city. Yet another factor people have pointed out is the asphalt overlaying all the roadways, which prevents pollen from being absorbed into the soil and allows it to continue swirling around in the air.

The marked rise in the number of allergy sufferers has led the **Japan Weather Association** to issue pollen count reports over the last decade.

Pollen is especially prevalent on fine dry days when a warm wind blows in from the southwest. On rainy days there is not nearly so much because of the high humidity.

**春の晴れた日は
花粉症患者の憂鬱な時**

ですからその日の天気・風向き・温度から花粉の飛ぶ量を推定し、「少ない、やや多い、多い、非常に多い」の4段階に分けて予報を出すようになったのです。

「花粉症」の人はこの予報を聞いてマスクなどをつけて自衛します。暖かく晴れ上がった春の日も、花粉症に悩む人たちにとっては憂鬱な時なのです。

日本ひとくち歳時記、今日は「花粉症」についてお話ししました。

Consequently, the determining factors in the pollen count on any given day in the pollen season are the weather, the wind direction and the temperature. There are four levels that the Japan Weather Association employs for its pollen count reports: low, rather high, high and extremely high.

These reports let pollen allergy sufferers know in advance whether to equip themselves with a mask or take other forms of precautionary measures. Warm, clear spring days can make hay fever sufferers feel very down in the **dumps**.

This has been *Around the Year in Japan*. On today's program we discussed *kafunshō*, or "hay fever."

駅　弁
Railway Station Box Lunches

日本ひとくち歳時記、今日は「駅弁」について
お話ししましょう。

This is *Around the Year in Japan*. Today we are
going to talk about *ekiben*, the box lunches sold
at stations.

日本人は、職場や学校の昼食は
もちろん、芝居見物、スポーツ
の観戦、ピクニックなどさまざまな機
会に弁当を食べます。自分で作る場
合もあれば、店で売られているものを
買うこともあります。もちろん弁当は
季節を選ぶものではありませんが、新
緑の映える春先に屋外の風にあたり
ながら食べるというのは、また、格別
の味わいがあります。

　今日お話しする駅弁というのは、
列車で旅行する人のために、駅で売
られている弁当のことです。鉄道を
使っての旅行の楽しみの一つに、こ
の駅弁をあげる人は少なくありませ
ん。大きな駅の中やプラットホームの
売店には、色とりどりの包装紙に包
まれた弁当が並んでいます。

The Japanese are very fond of *bentō*, or box lunches, and they eat them on numerous occasions—at the workplace, at school, at theatrical performances, at sports events, and, of course, especially on picnics. Box lunches can be made at home, but they can also be purchased at a store. Box lunches may be enjoyed at any time, whatever the season. Still, there is a special feeling to having them in early spring while sitting in the open air with fresh green leaves swaying overhead in a gentle breeze.

Ekiben, the particular kind of box lunch we are talking about today, are sold at train stations, and they are generally meant to be eaten on the train. Many people cite *ekiben* or railway station box lunches as one of the main pleasures of train travel. All major train stations will have a kiosk on the platform with an assortment of various kinds of *ekiben* wrapped in colorful paper.

出かけるときに買っていく人もいれば、行く先々で売っている目先の変わった駅弁を楽しみにしている人もいます。

一般的な駅弁の中身は？

ではごく普通のものを一つ買って中を見てみましょう。固い紙で作った箱を包んでいる包装紙をはずし、フタを開けると、ご飯を半分ほど詰めた残りのスペースに、ひとくちで食べられる大きさに作られたさまざまなおかずがぎっしりと詰まっています。**焼いた魚**の切り身、甘辛く煮付けた牛肉、鶏の唐揚げ、タマゴ焼き、漬物など、どれから箸をつけようかと迷ってしまうほどです。

窓の外の移り変わる景色を眺めながらつまんでいると「旅に出てきたなあ」という実感が湧いてくるのです。

駅弁の年間販売数は7000万個以上

現在、日本全国でどのくらいの駅弁が売られているのでしょうか。じつは、あまりに多すぎて実態はつかみ切れないというのが、実情です。

しかし、ある駅弁業者の団体では、駅の数にして300以上、種類は2500種類、年間の販売数は7000万個を超えるのではないかと話しています。い

Some people pick up a box lunch before they board the train, while others look forward to sampling box lunches on sale at a station along the way.

Let's purchase a typical *ekiben* and see what goodies are inside. Removing the colorful paper wrapped around the cardboard box and lifting the lid, we see a good portion of cooked rice taking up half the box, and the rest of the box packed with various delicacies in bite-sized pieces—slices of **broiled fish**, beef cooked in soy sauce and sugar, fried chicken, a mini-omelet, assorted pickled items and so on. So many tempting foods that it may be hard to make up your mind which to attack first with your chopsticks.

With occasional glances at the scenery flashing by outside, you pick out the tender morsels one by one, and gradually start to enjoy the fact that you are indeed taking a trip.

How many types of *ekiben*, you may ask, are available in Japan? The truth is, there are so many that it is hard to give an accurate answer.

One industry organization estimates that with more than 300 train stations throughout Japan selling *ekiben*, and about 2,500 varieties, annual sales must top 70 million box lunches, a figure which reflects the extent to

かにたくさんの日本人が、旅行の際に駅弁を食べるか、この数字だけでも分かると思います。

日本初の駅弁は宇都宮駅の握り飯

駅弁が誕生したのは、今から100年以上も前の1885年。東京と、北へ100キロほど離れた宇都宮の間に鉄道が開通した際に、宇都宮の駅で売られたのが最初の駅弁といわれています。もっとも、その中身は竹の皮に包んだ握り飯二つにたくあん二切れという簡単なものでした。

そして日本全国に鉄道網が拡がるに連れて、駅弁も各地の駅で販売されるようになり、それと共に、駅それぞれに各地方の特色を活かしたさまざまな内容の駅弁が数多く生まれてきました。

では、ここで、日本全国の駅弁のうち、ユニークな内容で人気の高い駅弁をいくつかご紹介しましょう。

まず、北海道南部の森駅のイカ飯弁当。これは小型のイカの中に米を入れて煮たもので、ご飯にイカの味がしみておいしいものです。

特に人気の高い弁当はイカ飯と釜飯

全国駅弁人気投票で、このイカ飯弁当と常に1、2位を競っているのが、群馬県横川駅の峠の釜飯。小さなお

which *ekiben* have become a much-loved feature of everybody's travel agenda.

Railway station box lunches first appeared more than a century ago, in 1885, when the train line linking Tōkyō with the city of Utsunomiya, 100 kilometers to the north, opened for service. The first *ekiben* on sale at Utsunomiya Station was a very simple affair—two **rice balls** seasoned with two sliced pieces of pickled *daikon* (a type of raddish), wrapped in bamboo leaves.

As Japan's rail system developed into a network that spread over the entire country, *ekiben* started to be sold in various other regions. Box lunches on sale at train stations also began to feature local delicacies, producing a multifarious variety in the contents of *ekiben*.

Here are just a few of the most distinctive and popular *ekiben* in Japan.

The *ikameshi bentō*, on sale at Mori Station in the southern part of Hokkaidō, usually tops the nationwide surveys of the most popular box lunch. It consists of small **squid** stuffed with rice and steamed, the rice being permeated by the tasty squid juices.

A strong contender is the *tōge no kamameshi bentō* sold at Yokokawa Station in Gunma Prefecture, in which mountain vegetables, chicken, shrimp and other delicious

釜の形をした**陶器の器**の中に山菜、鶏肉、海老などを炊き込んだご飯がぎっしりと詰まっています。

北陸地方、富山駅のマスの押し寿司。酢飯の上に薄く切った**マス**を乗せて押しをしたものです。

その他、松阪牛で有名な三重県松阪駅の駅弁には、もちろん松阪牛が入っていますし、**カキ**の名産地、広島の駅弁は、カキをご飯に炊き込んで、カキフライを添えたカキ飯弁当。日本のほぼ真ん中、鮎（あゆ）で有名な長良川の流れる岐阜駅の駅弁は、鮎寿司。

駅弁は日本の地方特産物の宝庫

お聞きのように、駅弁の多くはその**地方の特産物**を活かして作ってありますから、駅弁が旅の楽しみになるというのもうなずいていただけるのではないでしょうか。皆さんも、日本を鉄道で旅行する機会がありましたら、ぜひ駅で駅弁を買って味わってみてください。その土地の印象が、目、耳だけでなく、舌を通じても皆さんの心の中に残ると思います。

日本ひとくち歳時記、今日は「駅弁」についてお話ししました。

morsels are cooked with rice in a small **ceramic vessel** modeled after the wide-mouthed pot used to cook rice.

Another famous *ekiben* is the *masu no oshizushi*, sold at Toyama Station in the Hokuriku district. This consists of thin strips of **salmon trout** pressed into a bed of vinegared rice.

Other top choices include the box lunch sold at Matsuzaka Station in Mie Prefecture, which features the renowned local Matsuzaka beef; the *kaki bentō* of Hiroshima (an area famed for its **oysters**), with oysters cooked in rice and an extra topping of fried oysters; and the *ayu-zushi ekiben* of Gifu Station, in the center of Japan close to the Nagara River, which is famed for its *ayu* sweetfish.

As you will gather, most *ekiben* are designed to show off the **special delicacies of their locality**. I think we've probably managed to persuade our listeners into seeing why station box lunches have come to be considered part of the pleasure of travel. Should you have a chance to travel by train in Japan, we urge you to pick up a box lunch at a train station and sample its contents. That way, you will remember the places you visit not only from the sights and sounds you experience there, but also from the delicious tastes of foods.

This has been *Around the Year in Japan*. On today's program we discussed *ekiben*, the box lunches sold at stations.

ワサビ
Wasabi

日本ひとくち歳時記、今日は「ワサビ」について
お話ししましょう。

This is *Around the Year in Japan*. Today we are
going to talk about *wasabi*.

ワサビなしでは
考えられぬ日本食

日本料理の代表的なものをあげろといわれたら、その上位に必ず入るのが、寿司と刺身です。

刺身は、新鮮な魚を薄い切り身にして皿にきれいに並べたものです。魚は生です。簡単な料理ですね。でも、旨い刺身は、日本人にとって最高の贅沢の一つです。

寿司はもう少し手が込んでいます。酢を混ぜたご飯をひとくちで食べられる大きさに軽く握り、その上に魚の切り身をのせたもの。この魚も生です。

生の魚を食べる？「気持ち悪い」と思った方もきっと多いのではないでしょうか。

でもじつは、日本人だって刺身をそのまま食べるなんて気持ちが悪い

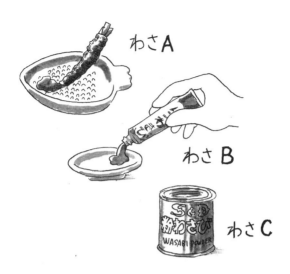

わさA

わさ B

わさ C

If we were asked to name an item typical of Japanese cuisine, *sushi* and *sashimi* would probably come at the top of the list.

Sashimi consists of thinly sliced pieces of very fresh raw fish arranged appealingly on a plate—the height of simplicity. Still, for Japanese, even simple *sashimi* is quite a delicacy—and it's one of the more expensive ways of eating seafood.

Sushi requires a bit more preparation than *sashimi*. It consists of small portions of rice mixed with a dash of **vinegar** and patted by hand into bite-sized pieces, and then topped with slices of fish or other seafood. The seafood used for *sushi* too is raw.

Raw fish? Quite a few of our listeners must find the idea of eating raw fish rather grotesque.

But the truth is, some Japanese also find the thought of eating *sashimi* alone somewhat unappealing. With

んです。寿司の方はいく分手が入っていますから、**気持ち悪い**というほどではありませんが、一番高価な**マグロ**のトロ（脂身の部分）を握った寿司をそのまま口に放り込むなんて、やっぱりあまりいい気持ちはしません。

では、それを日本人の最高の好物に変えるのはいったい何でしょう。それが、日本の代表的な**調味料**である醤油と、今日お話しするワサビなんです。醤油の方は最近では海外でも手に入りやすくなっていますから、味わった方もあるでしょうが、ワサビは皆さんのところではなかなか手に入らないのではないでしょうか。

ワサビは日本特産の草の一種

ワサビというのは、山間のきれいな冷たい水の流れる砂地に生える日本特産の、一種の草です。ワサビといわれてもあまり春という季節を感じる人はいないでしょうが、ちょうどいまごろ（4月ごろ）花茎（かけい）を生じ、小さな白色の花をつけます。長さ10センチほどの太い茎があり、これをすり下ろして使います。どんな味がするのでしょうか。

これだけの前置きをしたからには、きちんと説明したいのですが、じつはこれがなかなか説明が難しいのです。

sushi, since there is slightly more preparation involved, the **adverse feeling** is not quite so strong, but still, most people would not be too thrilled at the thought of popping *maguro no toro sushi* (a sushi made with a particularly fatty type of **tuna**) into their mouth without any condiment.

So what is it that transforms slices of raw fish into one of the most highly prized dishes in Japanese cuisine? The answer is *shōyu*, or soy sauce, one of the most popular Japanese **seasonings**, and *wasabi*, the subject of today's program. *Shōyu* is available pretty much everywhere nowadays, so I am sure many of our listeners are familiar with its taste. But fresh *wasabi*, on the other hand, is much more difficult to obtain unless you are in Japan.

Wasabi is a variety of herb similar to horseradish, which in Japan grows in sandy areas around cold, clear rivers and streams flowing deep in the mountains. There are few people for whom the mention of the word *wasabi* is suggestive of spring, but at this time of the year, around April, flower buds appear on *wasabi*, then it bears tiny white flowers. It has a thick stem that measures about 10 centimeters long, which can be grated and used for seasoning. And·what does it taste like?

I would dearly love to be able to give you a decent explanation, but the fact is, *wasabi*'s taste is nearly impossible to describe. It's a **fierce** taste that hits the

口に含んだ途端に鼻にツーンと抜ける**強烈な**香り、でもいやな香りではなくて、爽やかな香りを持っています。たいへん辛いのですが、自然な甘みも持っています。

すり下ろした薄緑色のペースト状のもの、ほんの少量を醤油といっしょに、刺身につけて口に入れると、さっき「気持ち悪い」なんていったいどこの誰が言ったの、というくらいに、味が一変して最高のご馳走に変わってしまうのです。寿司でしたら、ご飯と魚の間にほんの少々このワサビがつけられています。ワサビの効いた寿司、毎日でも食べたいという人さえいるほどです。

でもこの味が分かるのは、大人になってから。子供のころはあまりに刺激が強すぎるので、食べさせてもらえません。寿司を注文するときも、親は子供の分にはワサビを入れないように職人に頼みます。これを「サビ抜き」といいます。

サビ抜きというのは、子供扱いの代名詞で、子供向けの寿司とも言うべきものです。ですから、少し大きくなってワサビの入った寿司を口に入れ、その強烈な刺激で目から出る涙

ワサビが寿司を
ごちそうに変える

back of your nose almost as soon as you put it into your mouth—but it's not disagreeable, in fact, very refreshing. True, it is fiery hot, but it also has a naturally sweet tang.

As you dip the *sashimi* into a mixture of a small amount of soy sauce and the green paste made from freshly ground *wasabi*, then pop the *sashimi* into your mouth, you'll find the taste of the fish so delicious that you'll forget your previous opinion about raw fish being disgusting. With *sushi*, a dab of *wasabi* alone is placed in between the fish and the rice, producing such a mouth-watering delicacy that some people only wish they could eat it every day.

Wasabi is, however, an adult taste. Children find *wasabi* overly strong, so they are usually not given it to eat. When parents order *sushi* for their children, they usually tell the *sushi* chef to leave out the *wasabi*—this is referred to as *sabi-nuki*, which literally means "minus the *wasabi*."

Sabi-nuki has consequently come to mean "*sushi* for children." When a child reaches an age when he or she starts eating *sushi* made with *wasabi*, its strong taste will bring tears to the eyes, but at the same time there will be the compensation of finally being treated like an adult.

と共に、大人扱いになったのだという実感を味わうのです。

ワサビはなかなか手が出ない高価なもの

　ワサビは高価です。長さ10センチほどのものが1000円以上もしますから、家庭ではいつも口にするというわけには、なかなかいきません。そこで、家庭の食卓には、安く手に入るホースラディッシュ、ワサビ大根などを原料として作った粉ワサビやチューブ入りの練りワサビが登場するのが普通です。

　日本ひとくち歳時記、今日は「ワサビ」についてお話ししました。

Fresh *wasabi* is not cheap: a 10-centimeter piece costs 1,000 yen or more, so it is not eaten on a regular basis at home. Usually, for the family dining table a substitute such as powdered *wasabi* or prepared *wasabi* paste in a tube is used instead. These substitutes are made from inexpensive horseradish and Japanese *daikon* radish.

This has been *Around the Year in Japan*. On today's program we discussed *wasabi*.

山葵 わさび
アブラナ科の多年草。水が清く水温が低い山間の渓流(けいりゅう)にはえる。葉はアオイに似て、葉柄(ようへい)は長さ約30 cm。3〜5月に四弁の白花が開く。根茎を香辛料として用いるため、栽培もされる。葉・茎・根茎は、わさび漬け・辛味料にする。辛味は、シニグリンが加水分解され、からし油に変化して生じたもの。薬用にもされる。
山葵が利く(わさびがきく) 1: ワサビの味とかおりが強いこと。2: 人の心に、ぴりっとした、鋭い印象を与える。smart。
山葵を利かす(わさびをきかす) 1: ワサビの辛味・香味を十分に出させる。2: ぴりっと引き締まった言動をする。

日本茶
Green Tea

日本ひとくち歳時記、今日は「日本茶」について
お話ししましょう。

This is *Around the Year in Japan*. Today we are
going to talk about green tea.

**日に何杯も
お茶を飲む日本人**

日本人はよくお茶を飲みます。朝起きると目覚ましに1杯。会社について仕事を始める前に1杯。3時ごろ、軽い**お菓子**をつまんで1杯。その他食事の後には必ず飲みますから、1日6杯くらいは飲むのが普通です。

そんな日本人がお茶というときは、だいたい**緑茶**をさします。紅茶が、摘んだ葉をいったんしおれさせた後、よく揉み発酵させるのに対し、日本の緑茶は摘んだばかりの**芽葉**を蒸気で熱して酵素の働きを止めた後、数時間かけて揉んで乾燥させたものです。**葉緑素**が変化していないため、いれると鮮やかな緑色でさわやかな香りがあります。

お茶はわが国には、9世紀に中国か

Green Tea 飲むと
長生きするのよ

The Japanese are great drinkers of tea. One cup in the morning to get fully awake, another when they reach the office before settling down to work. Around three in the afternoon, another cup, perhaps with a light **sweet**. And definitely at least one cup of tea after every meal. On average, this probably means about six cups of tea every day.

But tea, or *ocha*, for Japanese usually inevitably means **green tea**. Whereas the other type of tea (*kōcha*, "red" tea in Japanese) is produced by a process involving partial fermentation, where the picked leaves are left to wither and then partly crushed to stimulate the fermenting process, with Japanese green tea, the **stems** and **leaves** are steamed as soon as the tea is picked, cutting off the fermentation process. They are then rubbed for several hours and thoroughly dried. This method prevents the natural **chlorophyll** in the leaves from undergoing chemical change, so it retains its vibrant green color and fresh fragrance.

Tea was introduced to Japan from China during the

ら入ってきました。最初は**薬用**として用いられ、煎じて飲んだり、粉にしたものを湯に溶いて飲んだりしていました。

　今のようにお湯で浸出(しんしゅつ)させて飲むようになったのは17世紀になってからですが、それでも贅沢な習慣とされ、庶民的な飲み物となったのは18世紀になってからのようです。

新茶とふつうのお茶はどこが違う?

　さて、ちょうど今ごろ、5月初旬になるとお茶屋さんの店先には「新茶入荷しました」という張り紙が目につくようになります。この新茶という言葉を聞くと日本人は「夏が来たのだなあ」と感じるのです。

　5月初旬に摘むお茶を一番茶、6月下旬に摘むのを二番茶、7月下旬に摘むのを三番茶といいます。摘む時期が早いほど**アミノ酸**の含有量が多いため、旨みがあり、後になるほど**タンニン**が多くなり渋みが強くなっていきます。新茶の高い香りと旨みは格別で、つい手が出てしまうという人も多いようです。

　では、ここで緑茶のおいしいいれ方をお教えしましょう。

9th century, and at first it was used for **medicinal purposes**, prepared by infusion or else in a powdered form mixed with boiled water.

It was only during the 17th century that people began to drink tea made according to the current method, with tea leaves being soaked in boiling water—and even so this was considered an extravagent way of enjoying the beverage and not adopted by the common people until the 18th century.

Around the beginning of May in Japan you start seeing notices put out in front of tea shops which say: "Shipments of New Tea Just Arrived." This "new tea," or *shincha*, makes most Japanese feel that finally summer is just around the corner.

The tea picked in early May is referred to as *ichiban cha* or "first tea." That picked in late June is *niban cha* or "second tea," while that picked at the end of July is *sanban cha* or "third tea." The earlier in the season, the more loaded the picked tea is with **amino acids**, and the more subtle the taste. The later in the season, the more **tannic acid** it contains, and the more astringent it is to the tongue. New tea has a particularly special aroma and flavor, so it is highly sought after and appreciated.

The following is one way of enjoying a cup of tasteful green tea.

塩分や鉄分の多い水を避け、なるべく深山に湧く清水のような**軟水**を沸騰させます。ポットに1人分当たりお茶の葉をスプーン1杯、お湯を100ミリリットルほど入れます。

上等なお茶は入れ方も違う

上等なお茶ほどお湯の温度は低く、長い時間をかけていれるのがよいとされています。もっとも上等な玉露という種類の場合、沸騰させた後50度から60度に冷ましたお湯を2分半ほど入れます。

日本人が緑茶を飲むときは「絶対に」砂糖やミルクは入れません。お茶だけの味を楽しみます。これはお茶の旨みと香り、そして緑の色と香りを味わうためです。日本人でも紅茶を飲むときは、逆に砂糖やミルク、レモン、ブランデーなどを入れる人が多く、何も入れずに飲む人の方が少なくなっています。

日本ひとくち歳時記、今日は「日本茶」についてお話ししました。

When you brew *shincha*, you should avoid water with a high salt or iron content; if possible you should use **soft water**, like that which flows in the clearest mountain streams. Into the teapot you put the appropriate amount of tea for the number of cups to be prepared, one spoon per cup, and add about 100 milliliters of boiled water.

The better the quality of the tea, the cooler the water can be allowed to get. The tea should then be left to steep for a short time in a pot. With the very finest tea, known as *gyōkuro* (literally, "jewel dew"), the water is boiled and left to cool to 50 or 60 degrees centigrade, and only then poured over the tea leaves, which should steep for about two and a half minutes.

When Japanese drink green tea, they never add sugar or milk: the flavor of the tea itself is what's important—that and the aroma, and the lovely green color. But with "red" tea, it's just the opposite: they tend to add all sorts of things, sugar, milk, lemon, brandy. In fact, very few Japanese drink *kōcha* straight.

This has been *Around the Year in Japan*. On today's program we discussed green tea.

夏 Summer

Part 2

カツオ
Bonito

日本ひとくち歳時記、今日は「カツオ」について
お話ししましょう。

This is *Around the Year in Japan*. Today we are
going to talk about *katsuo*, or "bonito."

カツオは黒潮に
のってやってくる

日本は島国ですから**海産物**が豊富
です。日本人は魚を好んでよく
食べるということをご存じの方も多い
ことでしょう。

日本人はいろいろな魚を食べます
が、代表的なものといえば、やはり、
マグロ、サケ、カツオ、イワシ、といっ
たところでしょうか。このうち、初夏
に話題にのぼるのがカツオです。

熱帯から温帯にかけての海にすむ
カツオは春の初めに日本の南岸沖に
姿を現し、**黒潮**と呼ばれる暖流にの
って南岸沿いを北上します。7〜8月
には東北地方沖に達し、秋になると
逆に南下を始めて11月ごろには日本
近海から姿を消します。

Japan is a country of islands, so it is rich in **marine products**. No doubt many of you know that the Japanese love to eat fish.

Many varieties of fish are consumed, most commonly **tuna**, **salmon**, **bonito**, and **sardines**. Among these, bonito is a fish particularly associated with summer, especially early summer.

Bonito live in tropical and temperate waters; during early spring, they make their first appearance off Japan's southern coasts, and gradually work their way northward up the coast, swimming in the warm **Black Current**. By July or August they reach the waters off the Tōhoku district in the northeastern part of Japan's main island of Honshū. When autumn comes, they reverse course and head south, disappearing from the country's coastal waters around November.

　春から夏にかけて北上する途中で捕獲される、その年の出回り初めのカツオは「初ガツオ」と呼ばれてとりわけ珍重されます。

　かつて江戸（今の東京）の町民たちは、魚でも野菜でも、その年初めて出荷されるものを特に好んだということですが、江戸時代の有名な俳句に「目には青葉　山ホトトギス初ガツオ」という句があるように、初ガツオは初夏の風物として代表的なものの一つに数えられています。

おすすめのカツオの食べ方は？

　さて、カツオの食べ方としては、何といっても刺身です。刺身は、**醤油**にワサビを溶かしたものにつけて食べることが多いのですが、カツオの場合は、ワサビの代わりに**ショウガ**、**ニンニク**、**刻みネギ**、**からし**などを加えます。

　また、表面を**火**で焙ってから冷やし、醤油、酢などを混ぜたタレで食べる「タタキ」、醤油で煮込む煮付けなどが一般的です。

　また、日本で捕れるカツオのうち40パーセントは、カツオブシという

The first bonito, taken as the fish progress northward during spring and summer, are referred to as *hatsugatsuo* or "the first bonito of the season," and they are highly prized.

In premodern times, the citizens of Edo, now Tōkyō, were especially fond of the first foods of the season to be offered on the market, and they were willing to pay hefty prices for them—vegetables as well as fish. A *haiku* poem from the Edo period (1600–1868) tells us much about the citizens' priorities: "For the eyes, the new green leaves of the trees; for the ears, the call of the cuckoo; for the mouth—the first catch of bonito." Bonito was clearly something that had an important association with people's experience of early summer days.

Most Japanese would probably opt to eat bonito as *sashimi*, or sliced raw fish. *Sashimi* is usually eaten dipped in a condiment of **soy sauce** and *wasabi*, but in the case of bonito, one eats it with grated **ginger**, **garlic**, **chopped green onion**, or **mustard**.

Another way of eating it involves the fish being **charred** on the surface, chilled and then served with soy sauce, vinegar or some other kind of dipping. This style is known as *tataki*. Yet another popular method of preparation involves boiling the fish in soy sauce.

Around 40 percent of the bonito caught in Japanese waters is used to make a food item known as *katsuo-bushi*.

加工品を作るのに使われます。「カツオブシ」は、カツオの切り身を茹でたあと火で焙り、さらに日に干して作る、日本独特の食品です。

ちょっと見たところ木のようで、とても堅く、そのまま食べることはできません。専用のカンナで、ちょうど木を削るように削って使います。

**吸物のダシに最適な
カツオブシ**

沸騰した湯に削ったカツオブシを入れて火を止めてこすと上等の**ダシ**がとれます。日本料理では、このカツオブシと昆布を使ったダシが吸い物に最適とされています。

日本ひとくち歳時記、今日は「カツオ」についてお話ししました。

This distinctively Japanese product is made by a process which involves first boiling large pieces of the fish, then roasting them, and then letting them dry in the sun.

At first sight, the dried chunks of fish resemble nothing so much as chunks of wood—and they become hard like wood, inedible in this form. For cooking, shavings of the dried fish are planed off the chunks with a special planing knife.

These shavings are first put in boiling water, which is then put through a straining cloth, to produce a fine translucent **broth**. This is used together with *konbu*, a kind of seaweed, and lies at the heart of the delicate soups in Japanese cuisine.

This has been *Around the Year in Japan*. On today's program we discussed *katsuo*, or "bonito."

鰹 かつお
サバ科の海水魚。暖海の表層にすむ典型的な回遊魚。全長40～60cm。背側は暗青色、腹部は銀白色。死後、腹部に数本の青い縦じまが出る。一本釣りが大半。刺身（さしみ）・かつおぶし用。土佐（とさ）のたたきが有名。世界の温帯・熱帯海域に分布。ショウギョ。bonito。**数え方**　一本・一尾（び）。

梅　雨
The Rainy Season

日本ひとくち歳時記、今日は「梅雨」について
お話ししましょう。

This is *Around the Year in Japan.* Today we are
going to talk about *tsuyu* or, the "rainy season."

梅雨は梅の実の
熟するころ始まる

日本の気候は、四季の気温の変化が比較的はっきりしていますが、乾季と雨季の明確な差はありません。ただ、6月から7月にかけての一月余りは特に雨の多い時期で、「つゆ」または「ばいう」と呼ばれます。

　漢字では「梅雨」と書きますが、これはちょうどこの時期に梅の実が**熟する**ことからきています。

　梅雨のころの典型的な**天気図**を見ますと、北方の冷たいオホーツク海**高気圧**と、南方の暖かい太平洋高気圧が日本付近で衝突して**停滞前線**を作っています。これは**梅雨前線**と呼ばれ、この前線の上を次々と**低気圧**が通過して雨を降らせます。

The temperature changes of the four seasons in Japan are comparatively clear cut. But rain falls throughout the year, and no one season is especially more rainy than another. However, there is a period lasting a little more than a month during June and July characterized by a lot of rainfall. This is the *tsuyu*, or "rainy season," sometimes referred to as *baiu*.

Both these words are written with a Chinese-character compound that literally means "apricot rain," which is appropriate since the period falls just at the time apricots **ripen**.

A look at typical **meteorological charts** in the rainy season shows a **stationary front** which is formed by warm Pacific Ocean high pressure systems from the south coming head to head with **high pressure systems** from the cold Okhotsk Sea in the north. This weather front is referred to as the **seasonal rain front**, and above it, one after the other, **low pressure systems** pass,

梅雨前線は南から北へと徐々に移動するので、梅雨の地域もそれにしたがって移動します。日本の最南端の沖縄地方は5月中旬に梅雨入りし、本州の東北部では6月中旬と約1ヵ月の差があります。

日本列島の最北の北海道は梅雨前線から外れているので梅雨はありませんが、朝鮮半島の南部と中国の長江流域では梅雨があります。

梅雨の雨はじとじとと毎日のように降り続きますが、梅雨も後期に入ると時には雷を伴う豪雨となって水害を引き起こすこともあります。梅雨の間の降雨量は、多い所では年間降雨量の3分の1にも達します。

**梅雨の時期の
カビ対策**

また、梅雨時の日本は高温多湿のためカビが生えやすいので注意が必要です。食べ物が腐りやすく食中毒を起こす原因ともなります。浴室など湿気の多い所では壁がカビで黒くなり、いくらこすってもなかなか取れません。

そのため、カビを防ぐスプレーと

depositing rain on the land and sea below them.

As the seasonal rain front progresses slowly from the south to the north, the apricot rains gradually shift from one region to the next in a northward pattern. The apricot rains hit the Okinawa region, the southernmost islands of Japan, in mid-May, but it is about one month later, in the middle of June, that the rains reach the Tōhoku region in northeast Honshū.

Hokkaidō, up in the northeast, is beyond the reach of the seasonal rain front, so it is not affected by the apricot rains. However, the rain does reach the southern part of the Korean Peninsula and the lower reaches of the Chiangjiang River in southern China.

The rain falls, or rather drips, damply day after day. Occasionally towards the end of the period, there are storms with violent thunder and **torrential downpours**, sometimes resulting in floods. In areas receiving particularly heavy rain during this season, the amount of rain can reach one-third of the total rainfall for the year.

During the rainy season particular attention in Japan has to be paid to **mold**—the **warm temperatures and high humidity** make it grow quickly. Food spoils easily too, which leads to frequent cases of **food poisoning** at this time. In parts of the house with high humidity, like bathrooms, the walls can get positively black with mold, which is sometimes impossible to eradicate through scouring alone.

For this reason, mold-prevention sprays and mold-

**梅雨は憂鬱な
ことばかりか?**

かカビ取り液が必需品です。浴室で使うプラスチック製品をはじめ、衣類や家具などにも、防カビ加工をしたものが盛んに売られています。

このように梅雨の時期は憂鬱なことが多くて嫌いだという人がほとんどですが、悪いことばかりではありません。この時期はまた、色とりどりのハナショウブや、花の色を緑から白、青紫色あるいは薄紅色へと変えていくアジサイなどが、梅雨の雨にうたれていっそう鮮やかに咲き誇り、私たちの目を楽しませてくれます。

日本ひとくち歳時記、今日は「梅雨」についてお話ししました。

removal fluids become indispensable household items at this time of year. A plethora of products is available to combat mold on items from plastic basins to clothing and furniture—just about anything you care to mention.

The rainy season is a **depressing** season for all these reasons, so nearly everyone dislikes it. But not everything about it is bad. For example, this is the time of year that the beautifully colored **irises** come into bloom, as do the **hydrangea**, whose flowers vary from light green to white, light purple or light pink. These and other flowers only display their full beauty in the light drizzle of the *tsuyu* rains.

This has been *Around the Year in Japan*. On today's program we discussed *tsuyu*, or the "rainy season."

梅雨 つゆ
夏至（げし）をはさんで前後20日、6月10日ごろから7月10日ごろまで、約40日ぐらいの雨期。梅雨前線の停滞でおこる。ばいう。

梅干し
Pickled Apricots

日本ひとくち歳時記、今日は「梅干し」について
お話ししましょう。

This is Around the Year in Japan. Today we are
going to talk about *umeboshi*, or "pickled apricots."

古くから庭木として愛されてきた梅

日本の花といえば、まずなんといっても桜ですが、その桜が咲く前の冬枯れた庭で、「もう冬も終わり、もうじき春ですよ」と教えるように咲くのが梅です。

桜ほどには華やかではありませんが、**香りが高く**、古くから庭木として愛好されてきました。梅は花を楽しむだけでなく、実も、**食用**、薬用としてさまざまに使われてきました。

その中でも最も代表的なものが梅干しです。

梅干しが書物に初めて現れるのは8世紀末ですから、それ以前から食されていたと考えられます。地方によって大きく異なる日本の風土とともに育ってきましたから、作り方も土地によってさまざまですが、簡単にいえ

The cherry blossom, or *sakura*, is probably most Japanese people's favorite flower, but it's the apricot that puts forth delicate blossoms well before the cherry, in bare wintertime gardens, as a sign to tell us that spring is just a step away.

Though not as gorgeous and showy as the cherry blossom, the apricot blossom is very **fragrant**, and from ancient times it has been a favorite in Japanese gardens. The apricot is appreciated not only for its flowers but also for its fruit, used for various **culinary** and medicinal purposes.

The most common way in which the fruit is used is in *umeboshi*, or "pickled apricots."

The first written reference to *umeboshi* occurs in a record from the late 8th century, but it is thought that they were eaten even prior to that time. Since then the ways of pickling apricots have developed in accordance with the wide differences in lifestyles that existed in Japan in different localities. Generally, the procedure

ば、梅の塩漬けを半ば乾燥させたものが梅干しです。

日本列島が梅雨に入る6月上旬、梅の実は急に大きくなります。緑色だった実が黄色く色づき出すころを選んで収穫し、実の重さの20パーセントから25パーセントもの塩を使って塩漬けにします。4〜5日すると、やや黄色みを帯びた酢が出てきます。これは「梅酢」と呼ばれ、薬用に用いられてきました。

さて、この梅酢が出てから3〜4週間ほど置いた後、赤ジソの葉を容器に入れて赤い色をつけます。そして夏の暑い盛りになったら、梅を取り出して天日で、3日3晩干し上げます。夜の間は梅酢の中に戻すというやり方もあります。干し上がった梅に再び梅酢を加え、重石をして冷暗所に保存すると、半年ぐらいで梅干しができあがります。

梅干しは非常に保存性が高く、**10年**ぐらいは十分に保存できますし、状態が良ければ100年以上前のものでも大丈夫といいます。時々、古い家を整理していて江戸時代の梅干しが

**梅は梅雨と共に
急に成長する**

involves steeping the apricots in sea salt for a while, and then setting them out to dry.

From early June, the start of the *tsuyu* (literally "apricot rains") season in Japan, the fruit of the apricot suddenly gets very big. As soon as the apricots, originally bright green, start to acquire a yellowish hue, they are picked and put in a pot to steep for a while in sea salt, in a ratio of about one part salt to four or five parts fruit. In four days or so, a yellow juice seeps out of the apricots. This is known as *umezu*, or "apricot vinegar," and is used for its medicinal properties.

The apricots are then left for another three to four weeks, after which red *akajiso* leaves are added to the pickled apricots to give them, eventually, a reddish coloring. When the full heat of summer arrives, the apricots are taken out and allowed to dry in the sun for three days and three nights, though some people return the apricots to their vinegar at night. When the fruit is thoroughly dried, it is again returned to the vinegar, and a heavy stone is placed on top of the container, which is then stored in a cool place. In about half a year, the pickled apricots will be ready to eat.

Pickled apricots can be preserved for a remarkable length of time, and they remain edible for at least a **decade**. In fact, it is said that if the conditions are right, pickled apricots can remain edible for more than a century. From time to time, we hear news reports about old

出てきて、それが十分に**食べられる**状態だったというニュースが放送されることすらあるほどです。

梅干しの持つ さまざまな効用

　梅干しは、ご飯といっしょにそのまま食べる他、和え物や煮物、漬物、お菓子などの味付けにも用いられます。酒飲みの中には、お湯で割った焼酎に梅干しを入れるのを好む人もいます。

　また、暑い季節にお弁当のご飯に添えると、色どりはもちろんのこと、ご飯が傷みにくいという効用もあります。これは梅干しに**クエン酸、リンゴ酸**などが含まれているためです。

　さらに食欲増進の作用もありますから、夏バテのときには不可欠です。いずれにしても夏と梅干しは切っても切れません。

　これ以外にも、胃腸を整えるとか、疲労回復などの作用もあり、古くから薬用に用いられています。

　皆さんのお国ではなかなか梅干しを口にすることはないでしょうが、日本へ来たときなどには目にすることもあると思います。

houses being torn down to build new ones, and discoveries of still **edible** pickled apricots from the Edo period (1600–1868).

Pickled apricots are used as a simple pickle to go with cooked rice, but they are also used in various ways for flavoring, for example in vegetable side dishes, other kinds of pickles, and confectioneries. Drinkers sometimes enjoy them with alcoholic beverages, for example, plopped into a glass of distilled spirits cut with hot water.

Pickled apricots are also useful in summer box lunches, where besides providing a colorful decoration for the rice they also act to prevent it from going bad—pickled apricots contain **citric acid** and **malic acid**, which inhibit food spoilage.

Japanese people eat pickled apricots when they loose appetite, especially during hot days in summer, knowing that pickled apricots help to stimulate their stomachs. In this aspect pickled apricots are an indispensable food in summer.

In addition, pickled apricots have been much prized since ancient times for their medicinal properties, including the ability to heal stomach ulcers and help people recover from fatigue.

It's probably quite difficult for most of our listeners to get hold of pickled apricots to sample. But if you've made a trip to Japan, you must know what we're talking about.

　でも、いきなり梅干しを一つ口に放り込むなどということはしないでください。あまりの酸っぱさに、しかめた顔がしばらく元に戻らなくなってしまうかもしれませんから。

　それほど酸味が強い食べ物ですから、その酸っぱさに慣れている日本人でも「梅干し」という名前を聞いただけで、口の中に唾が湧いてくるほどなのです。

　日本ひとくち歳時記、今日は「梅干し」についてお話ししました。

Be careful, though, not to just pop a whole one into your mouth—you may be in for a shock. Pickled apricots are very salty and sour, so sour that your mouth may shrivel up in shock and not return to its natural state for some time.

Even Japanese people, who know all about this sourness, feel the **saliva gush** into their mouths at the mere mention of the word.

This has been *Around the Year in Japan*. On today's program we discussed *umeboshi*, or "pickled apricots."

梅干[し]
梅の実を塩漬けにしたあと日光で乾燥してアカジソとともに梅酢に漬けた食品。昔から薬用・保存食用。**数え方** 一個。

ボーナス
Semiannual Bonuses

日本ひとくち歳時記、今日は「ボーナス」について
お話ししましょう。

This is *Around the Year in Japan*. Today we are
going to talk about the bonus system in Japan.

日本のボーナスは
賃金の一部?

日本では公務員も含めて大多数のサラリーマンが、夏と冬の年2回ボーナス（賞与）を受け取ります。夏のボーナスはほとんどの会社で、6月半ばから7月の初めごろ支給されます。

本来、ボーナスというと仕事の上で標準以上の成果を上げた社員に、その報酬として支払われる割り増し賃金のことをさしますが、日本でのボーナスは、その意味あいが薄れ、ほとんど賃金の一部になっています。

特に第2次大戦後は、給与を補う生活補給金として、**労使交渉**で支給額が決められることが一般化しています。

ボーナスの支給額は企業の業種や、

In Japan the vast majority of salaried workers (including civil service employees), commonly referred to as *salaryman*, receive bonuses twice a year, in summer and winter. At most firms, the summer bonus is paid some time between the middle of June and the beginning of July.

The word "bonus" in its originally sense refers to a reward given to workers whose achievement and dedication have exceeded the norm—as a supplement to their regular salaries. However, in Japan that original meaning has been lost, and the bonuses are generally regarded as a part of a worker's regular compensation.

Particularly after the end of World War II, bonuses came to be considered a necessary addition to regular salaries—something like a cost of living allowance—and the amount of the bonuses at a company is determined through **management-labor negotiations**.

Although the amounts for the bonuses vary by

個々の会社の業績によって違いますが基本給の2〜2.5倍ぐらいが平均相場のようです。

　労働省労政局の調べによりますと、民間主要企業の1996年の夏期一時金は、平均77万3481円で、前年比3.3パーセント増となり、小幅ながら増えました。

**ボーナスの使い途は
人さまざま**

　ボーナスの使い途は人によってさまざまですが、給料以外のまとまったお金が入りますから、車や耐久家電製品、家具などの購入に充てたり、夏休み中の家族旅行の費用に充てたりします。

　もちろんバッチリ貯金にまわすという人も少なくありません。ボーナスシーズンは、デパートや大手スーパーなどの稼ぎ時で、バーゲンセールがあちこちで催されます。

　ボーナスが出る2、3ヵ月前からボーナス払いということで、品物先渡しの商戦をしている所もたくさんあります。もっとも、**住宅ローン**やその他のローンの返済に、あらかたボーナスが消えてしまうと嘆いている向きも、あるようですが。

industrial sector and according to the business results of the company concerned, normally the bonus will be equivalent to a worker's pay for between two and two-and-a-half months.

According to a survey in the summer of 1996 conducted by the **Labor Relations Bureau** of the **Ministry of Labor**, bonuses in private-sector companies averaged 773,481 yen, a slight increase of 3.3 percent over the year before.

The ways in which people like to use their bonuses vary. Since the bonus comes in one lump sum, some people use it to make large purchases—of motor vehicles, durable electric and electronic appliances, furniture and other high-ticket items. They may also use their bonus to take the family on trips during summer vacation.

Of course, quite a few people prefer simply to put the money straight into their bank account. Not surprisingly, bonus payment season is also a time of high earnings for department stores, large supermarkets and other retail stores, which often hold sales to lure in customers.

Many stores start sales wars two or even three months before bonuses are due, offering immediate take-home deals to be settled when the bonuses are paid. Often, however, we hear stories of people complaining that their bonuses are eaten up by **mortgages** and other kinds of loans.

**ボーナスを初めて
出した会社は?**

ところで、ボーナスを日本で初めて出したのは、三菱商事の前身である三菱商会で、明治9年、（1876年）のことといいます。当時のお金にして平社員で5円だったそうです。今の金額にすると3万円ぐらいでしょうか。

もっとさかのぼると、江戸時代に商店や職人の**親方**の所で働く**奉公人**に、盆、暮れに帯や着物などを支給していた、といいますから、これが日本のボーナスの始まりといえるかもしれません。

日本ひとくち歳時記、今日は「ボーナス」についてお話ししました。

Incidentally, the very first Japanese company to pay bonuses is generally thought to have been Mitsubishi Shōkai, the forerunner of today's Mitsubishi Corporation, which instituted the practice in 1876. The average worker at the company was presented with a bonus of 5 yen, the equivalent of about 30,000 yen today.

In fact, though, in the Edo period (1600–1868), there was a practice of presenting store clerks or **apprentices** who worked under **head artisans** with *obi* belts, kimono and other clothes in midsummer and at year's end. So it's probably truer to say that this custom was the origin of the bonus system in Japan.

This has been *Around the Year in Japan.* On today's program we discussed the bonus system in Japan.

ボーナス
1: 通常の賃金のほかに夏期・年末などに支給される特別手当。賞与。2: 割増金。株式の特別配当金。

七　夕
The *Tanabata* Star Festival

日本ひとくち歳時記、今日は「七夕」について
お話ししましょう。

This is *Around the Year in Japan*. Today we are
going to talk about the *Tanabata* Star Festival.

**七夕は中国の
古い伝説に由来**

7月の初め、日本では家々の軒先に長さ1メートル半から2メートルほどの**竹の枝**が立てられているのを目にすることがあります。枝のあちこちには色とりどりの紙の飾りがついています。

　これは7月7日に行われる「たなばた」という星祭りの行事のための笹飾りで、子供たちはこの日、さまざまな願い事を紙の短冊に書いて枝に吊るします。

　「七夕」はもともとは**陰暦**の7月7日に行われていた行事で、中国の古い伝説に由来するといわれています。中国近辺ではこの季節、夜空を見上げると、**天の川**をはさんで「鷲座（わし）」と「琴座（こと）」の2つの**星座**が輝いているのが見えます。

In the first week of July, you will often see a **bamboo branch** about one meter and a half to two meters in length standing out in front of Japanese homes. Its leaves will be adorned with all sorts of colorful paper decorations.

These paper decorations of bamboo are known as *sasakazari* and are used to celebrate the *Tanabata* Star Festival, which is held on July 7. On this day, youngsters write down various wishes on slips of paper and hang them from the bamboo branches.

The *Tanabata* Star Festival was originally a festival held on July 7 of the **lunar calendar**, and derives from an ancient Chinese legend. During this time of year if we look up into the night sky from the lands around China, we can see two particularly bright **constellations** (known in Chinese astronomy as the Eagle and the Harp) twinkling on either side the **Milky Way**.

この「鷲座」の一番明るい星である牛飼い星と「琴座」の一番明るい星の織女星（しょくじょ）は仲の良い夫婦でしたが、牛飼い星はアルタイル、織女星はベガとも呼ばれる星ですが、みなさんの国ではなんと呼ばれているのでしょうか?

あるとき神の**怒り**に触れ、天の川の対岸に別れ別れにさせられてしまいました。しかし年に1度、7月7日の夜、かささぎが一列にならんで天の川に橋を架け、2人が会うことができると言い伝えられています。

この**伝説**にちなんで中国では7月7日の夜にこの二つの星をまつって、願い事や**占い**をするという行事が行われるようになりました。

宮廷行事として始まった日本の七夕

この行事が、8世紀ごろには日本の宮廷の行事に取り入れられ、その後、日本の古い**伝承**などと結びついて独特の祭りとなったのです。

庶民の間に広く普及したのは17世紀、江戸時代になってからです。今では「七夕」の笹飾りは日本の夏の代表的な風物詩の一つとなっています。

もっとも近年は都会などでは**竹林**があまり見られなくなったこともあり、家庭で笹飾りをする家はめっきり減

The brightest star in the first constellation is the "Cowherd Star," while the brightest in the second is the "Weaver Star." Incidentally, in the West these two stars are known respectively as Altair and Vega. What are their names in your country?

According to the Chinese legend, the cowherd and weaver were once a very happily married couple but they incurred the **wrath** of a certain deity, and so were driven apart in the sky. Once a year, though, on the evening of July 7, birds form a bridge across the Milky Way for the couple to reunite.

In China, out of this **legend** a tradition developed of worshipping and making wishes to the two stars and practicing **divination**.

These practices were adopted by Japan's Court in the 8th Century, and they then became intertwined with aspects of Japan's indigenous **folklore** into a festival in its own right.

It became widely popular among the **common people** in the Edo period (1600–1868), and nowadays *sasakazari*, the decoration used at *Tanabata*, is a word typically associated with summer in Japan.

In recent years, **bamboo groves** have become much harder to find, especially in urbanized areas of the country, and the number of families displaying these decora-

ってきています。その一方、各地の都市や商店街では「七夕」を恒例行事として盛大に行う所が増えてきています。一種の客寄せ**作戦**というわけです。

日本の有名な2つの七夕祭り

このうちもっとも有名なのが関東地方の神奈川県平塚市と東北地方の宮城県仙台市です。平塚では7月初旬に、仙台では梅雨のシーズンを避けて8月初旬に行われ、色鮮やかな笹飾りを眺めて夏の訪れを満喫しようと、日本全国から200万人を超える観光客が押し寄せます。

日本ひとくち歳時記、今日は「七夕」についてお話ししました。

tions has declined markedly. On the other hand, more and more shopping arcades in towns and cities around the country have turned *Tanabata* into a regular public event and celebrate it as a **strategy** to attract shoppers and sightseers.

The most famous *Tanabata* festivals are those in Hiratsuka City in Kanagawa Prefecture, near Tōkyō, and Sendai City in Miyagi Prefecture, northeastern Japan. The festival in Hiratsuka is held at the beginning of July, while Sendai holds its event early in August so as to avoid the *tsuyu*, or early summer rains. Altogether the two festivals draw more than two million people from all around Japan, eager to view the decorations and enjoy the feeling that summer has truly arrived.

This has been *Around the Year in Japan*. On today's program we discussed the *Tanabata* Star Festival.

七夕 たなばた
1: 織機。また、それで布を織ること。織る人。loom; weaving; weaver。2: はたを織る女性。棚機津女（つめ）。woman weaver。3: 織女（しょくじょ）星。Vega。4: 五節句の一つ。また、その行事。年に一度会うという牽牛（けんぎゅう）星・織女星に婦女子が技芸の上達を祈願する。中国の乞巧奠（きこうでん）が日本に伝来したもの。七夕の節句。七夕祭り。しちせき。the Star Festival。

おばけ
Ghosts

日本ひとくち歳時記、今日は日本の「おばけ」について
お話ししましょう。

This is *Around the Year in Japan*. Today we are
going to talk about some of Japan's *obake*, or
"ghosts."

日本の夏とおばけは 切っても切れない

日本では、夏になると、「おばけ」が登場するお芝居や映画がしばしば上演、上映されます。また、遊園地の「おばけ屋敷」の人気も上昇します。

なぜ夏になると「おばけ」が注目されるのかというと、こわくて背筋がゾ〜ッと寒くなり、暑さを忘れるからという説もあります。

また、日本では夏に先祖の霊を迎える行事が行われるので幽霊が登場しやすい雰囲気だからという説を唱える人もいます。

「おばけ」には大きく分けると2種類あるといわれています。

With the arrival of summer in Japan, *obake*, or ghosts and other supernatural creatures, suddenly make an appearance in stage plays, movies and other forms of entertainment. At **amusement parks** the number of visitors to *obake-yashiki*, or haunted houses, soars.

The reason such spooky forms of entertainment become so popular during this season is that it is commonly believed that nothing is so effective as a good dose of **spine-tingling** terror to make one forget the hot muggy summer weather.

Some people also explain it by citing the fact that summer is the time Japanese believe the **souls of their ancestors** return to their family homes, and there are rites welcoming them back, and it is the time when Japanese visit their family graves. A general atmosphere prevails that makes it easy for ghosts to be around.

In general, *obake* can be divided into two categories.

一つは「幽霊」で、人に**恨み**を抱いたまま、あるいは何か思い残すことがあって亡くなった人が生前の姿のままで主に家族や知人の前に**現れたもの**です。

もう一つは「妖怪」で、こちらはもともと人間ではなく、**超自然**の存在で、特に相手を選ばず現れるといわれています。

幽霊と妖怪は どこが違う？

このうち「幽霊」はたいてい似たような姿で登場します。振り乱した長い髪、**額**には小さな白い三角形の紙をつけています。白い経帷子（きょうかたびら）を身に着け、両手は肘を曲げて胸の前で寄せるようにして、手首から先は**だらりと**下げています。そして足はなく宙に浮かんでいます。幽霊が現れる一番典型的な場所は川べりの**柳の木**の下ということになっています。

多くの幽霊は、「うらめしや～」と言いながら登場します。一般に幽霊は恨みを晴らすと姿を消します。

一方、「妖怪」のほうはいろいろな種類があります。よく知られたものをい

First there are the *yūrei* ghosts. These are **apparitions** of people who have died bearing some kind of **grudge** against a living person or with some fixed idea that keeps them attached to the land of the living. When they appear, they do so looking much as they were when alive, and usually to family members or acquaintances.

Then there are *yōkai*. These particular apparitions can take various forms, but they all share the common feature of never formerly having been human beings— their existence is fundamentally **supernatural**. They are also not particularly choosy about whom they appear to.

When *yūrei* appear, they generally display certain common features—long, disheveled hair, for example, a small triangular piece of white paper stuck on their **fore-heads**. They wear the white vestments for the dead, and they usually hold their arms up in front of their chests, bending them at the elbows, their hands drooping **limply**. What's more, they have no feet, so they appear to float through the air. The place a *yūrei* is most likely to appear is under a **willow tree** near a riverbank.

When a *yūrei* comes out, he or she usually wails something to the effect that "Oh, I'm bitterly, bitterly offended!" In most cases, after a ghost has related why it is so resentful, it disappears.

The *yōkai*, on the other hand, are a more diverse lot. To mention just a few of the most well known, first

くつかあげると、「一つ目小僧」…その名のとおり、目が一つしかありません。

「ろくろっくび」…首が長く伸びて空を飛びます。「のっぺらぼう」…顔に目鼻も口もなくつるりとしています。「海坊主」…海の中に棲み、黒くて頭の丸い、**ヌルヌル**した身体の巨大な怪物。

その他、「化け猫」など動物の姿をしたものとか、人の顔をしてニヤッと笑う花をつけた「人面樹」のような樹木の妖怪もあります。また、道の真ん中に突然壁が出現して通れなくなる時は、「塗り壁」という妖怪の仕業です。

このような妖怪の数は日本全国で500種類にのぼるといわれています。

おばけは時代の変わり目に流行する

ところで「おばけ」の研究家によりますと、時代の変わり目や**世紀末**になると「おばけ」に対する関心が高まるということで、日本で言えば江戸時代の末期、すなわち近代国家の幕開けとされる**明治維新**の直前にも妖怪ブームがありました。

また、世紀末であるここ数年も妖怪や**超自然の出来事**をテーマにした漫画や映画が人気を集めています。

there is the *hitotsume kozō*, or One-eyed Goblin—a monster with, as its name suggests, a single eye.

Then there is the *rokurokkubi*, a monster with a long neck who darts around in the air. There is the *noppera-bō*, a slippery monster with no eyes, nose, or mouth, and a giant sea monster known as *umibōzu*, which has a black, round head and a **slimy** body.

Besides these, there are various *obake* based on animals, like the *bake neko*, or Monster Cat, and also the *jin-menju*, a tree that bears flowers with grinning human faces. If you were walking down a road and suddenly found your way blocked by a wall that appeared out of nowhere, this would be the work of a *yōkai* known as the *nurikabe*, or Plaster-wall Monster.

All in all, Japan is said to be teeming with more than 500 varieties of such *yōkai*.

According to researchers of *obake*, interest in ghosts and monsters tends to increase during times of transition, such as the passage of a particular era or at the **end of a century**. In Japan's case, a big boom in *obake* occurred towards the end of the Edo period (1600–1868) when Japan was facing up to the fact of having to open up to the rest of the world, just before the **Meiji Restoration**.

As we near the end of our own century, *manga* cartoons, movies and other media featuring *yōkai* and **supernatural phenomena** are enjoying a great boom

皆さんのお国ではいかがでしょうか?

　日本ひとくち歳時記、今日は「お
ばけ」についてお話ししました。

once again in Japan. Is the same true in the countries of our listeners?

This has been *Around the Year in Japan.* On today's program we discussed Japan's *obake*, or "ghosts."

おばけ
1: 妖怪変化（ようかいへんげ）。幽霊。奇怪なもの。ばけもの。
monster; ghost。2: 形態などが異常に大きいもの。monster。

盆踊り
Bon Dance

日本ひとくち歳時記、今日は「盆踊り」について
お話ししましょう。

This is *Around the Year in Japan*. Today we are
going to talk about *Bon Odori*, or "*Bon* Dance."

**盆踊りは
日本の夏の風物詩**

真夏の夜、大太鼓の軽快なリズムにのった歌声が流れてきます。太鼓は、**お寺の境内**、公園、小学校の校庭など、街の空き地に組み上げられた**やぐら**の上で打ち鳴らされています。ちょうちんの赤い灯りに、やぐらの周りで踊る浴衣姿の老若男女が浮かび上がります。

8月15日前後、日本全国の交通機関は故郷に帰省する人々で大変な混雑となります。古来、日本人は、亡くなった先祖がこの時期になるとあの世から戻ってくると考えていました。

この**土着**の祖先信仰に、サンスクリット語でullambanaと呼ばれる盂蘭盆会の法要がいっしょになって、今の日本独特の仏教行事、「お盆」が

On the **midsummer** night breeze, singing and the cheerful rhythmic boom of large drums reach our ears: they're the unmistakable sounds of the *Bon* dance. The drums, or *taiko*, are set up on **scaffolds** in **temple precincts**, parks, elementary school playgrounds and other open areas, and under the red light of lanterns, people dressed in *yukata* summer kimono—young, old, men and women—dance in a giant circle.

Since ancient times the Japanese have believed that August is the time the souls of dead family members return briefly from the other world. Around August 15, mass transportation all over Japan is packed with people returning to their villages and homes in the country to be with them.

This practice derived from the **indigenous** faith involving ancestor worship which merged with a Buddhist festival known in Sanskrit as *ullambana*, or the "Festival of the Dead," the equivalent of All Souls' Day in the Christian

行われるようになりました。都会に働きに出た子供、親類たちもこの時期にはふるさとに集まり、あの世から訪れた祖先といっしょの時間を過ごすのです。

お盆は家族で先祖の霊を迎え入れる日

家の中に置かれた**仏壇**には、野菜や果物、お菓子のほか、**ナス**や**キュウリ**で作った馬や牛など、お盆独特の品が飾られます。馬や牛は祖先が戻ってくる時に乗る乗り物です。夕方になると、祖先が道を間違えずにこられるように、家の入り口で迎え火と呼ばれる火をたき、先祖の霊を家に迎え入れます。

そして、**僧侶**に**お経**をあげてもらい、あるいは**お墓**参りなどして先祖の霊を慰めます。こうしたお盆行事の中心の一つが盆踊です。子孫をはじめ、この世の人といっしょに踊ってひとときを楽しんでもらい、あの世に帰ってもらおうというのです。

盆踊りが、今のような形で踊られるようになったのは15世紀ごろといわれています。その後、さまざまな盆踊り歌が作られ、江戸時代に入って全

tradition. The festival of *O-Bon* in August fuses these Japanese and Indian traditions into a distinctly Japanese Buddhist festival. During *O-Bon*, members of the family who have left to work in the city head back to villages to commune with the souls of their ancestors returning temporarily from the other world.

The *butsudan*, or family **Buddhist altars** found in homes, are at this time laden with special *O-Bon* offerings, including vegetables, fruits and confections. **Eggplants** and **cucumbers** are fashioned into cows and horses for the souls of the dead to ride when they come for their summertime visit. When evening falls, a small welcoming fire is lit before the gate of each house to guide the souls of the dead home.

During the days of *O-Bon*, various things are done to comfort the souls of the departed. **Buddhist priests** may be asked to recite **sutras**, and the family will also pay a visit to the family **grave**. The *Bon* dance is an important part of these events: the idea is to provide the souls of the dead with entertainment, a chance to enjoy a dance with the living, their children and grandchildren, before sending them back to the other world.

It is said that the *Bon odori* as we know it today appeared around the 15th century. Since then various *Bon* melodies have developed, and during the Edo period (1600–1868), local areas throughout the country evolved

国各地に独自の郷土色を持った盆踊りが生まれるようになりました。大阪の河内音頭、岐阜の郡上踊り、秋田の西馬音内盆踊り、沖縄のエイサーなどは、多くの観光客を集めて盛んに行われています。

有名な阿波踊りも盆踊りの一つ

「踊る阿呆に見る阿呆、同じ阿呆なら踊らにゃ損々」。こんな歌詞と、三味線、太鼓、笛などの賑やかな囃子に乗って、自由奔放に踊りまくることで知られている徳島県の「阿波踊り」も、盆踊りの一つです。

徳島市民の多くが、「連」と呼ばれる数十人からなるグループを作って、町のあちこちで本番前から、練習を重ねます。そして8月中旬の数日間、200以上もの「連」が、昼から夜まで徳島市内を熱狂的な踊りの渦に巻き込むのです。

日本ひとくち歳時記、今日は「盆踊り」についてお話ししました。

their own unique dances. Some of the more famous ones, such as the *Kawachi Ondo* in Ōsaka, the *Gujō Odori* of Gifu Prefecture, the *Nishimonai Bon Odori* of Akita Prefecture, and the *Eisaa* of Okinawa, have become major tourist attractions.

"You're a fool to dance, and a fool to watch the dancing fools. So if you're going to be a fool, why not be a dancing fool?" This is the refrain that participants in the famous *Awa Odori* of Tokushima Prefecture on the island of Shikoku sing as they dance with abandon to the lively sounds of *shamisen*, drums and flute.

In Tokushima City there is a huge parade of *O-Bon* dancers. Residents get together in groups of a dozen or more dancers, or *ren*, and all over town people practice their dancing from well before the day of the actual event. For several days in mid-August you can see these groups, numbering more than 200 in total, dancing fervently and devotedly from morning till night.

This has been *Around the Year in Japan*. On today's program we discussed *Bon odori*, or "*Bon* Dance."

盆踊[り]
盂蘭盆（うらぼん）の踊り。祖霊祭りの盆行事と念仏踊りが合体した死者の霊を送るもの。一般に、櫓（やぐら）の周囲を輪踊りする形をとる。室町時代以降に普及した。

浴衣
Yukata

日本ひとくち歳時記、今日は「浴衣」について
お話ししましょう。

This is *Around the Year in Japan*. Today we are
going to talk about the garment known as *yukata*,
the informal summer kimono.

**浴衣は最近の若い
女性にも大人気**

日本人、ことに若い世代の人た
ちが、着物を着る機会は減り
続けています。成人式や卒業式、結
婚式などの冠婚葬祭以外の時に、着
物姿の若者たちを見かけることはほ
とんどないくらいです。一つ例外が、
ここ数年若い女性を中心に人気の出
ている「浴衣」です。

浴衣はもともとは湯上がりに着て
涼む木綿地のくつろぎ着でした。今
も、日本旅館やビジネスホテルには、
くつろぎ着として、あるいはパジャマ
代わりに着るために必ず備えてありま
す。「浴衣」はまた、街着にはならな
いけれど、夕涼み、縁日、盆踊りな
ど、夕方の散歩用に、以前から着用
されてきました。

しかし、日本人の衣生活の変化を

There are fewer and fewer opportunities nowadays for Japanese, especially younger Japanese, to wear kimono. Apart from very formal occasions, such as the **Coming-of-Age Ceremony** in January, **commencement exercises** and weddings, one hardly ever sees a young Japanese person dressed in a kimono. One exception is the increasing popularity in recent years, especially among young women, of the *yukata*.

The *yukata* started out as a simple loose-fitting cotton robe a person put on after coming out of the bath, to cool off and lounge around in. Even today at traditional inns (*ryōkan*) and business hotels, *yukata* are always provided for the guests to stroll around in or to use in place of pajamas. Although the *yukata* is not daily **street wear**, people do go out in *yukata* for a cooling evening stroll, to attend festivals and to dance in during the season for the *Bon* dance, and so on.

For a time *yukata* production declined steadily,

反映して、浴衣の生産はずっと減り続けていました。ところが、90年代に入って、若い女性の間で夏のお洒落着として「浴衣」が見直され、ちょっとしたブームが起こっています。花火大会や、パーティーに浴衣で出かけるのが流行っているのです。

昔と今では浴衣の好みも大きく違う

浴衣のデザインや**配色**も、若者たちの好みを反映して変わってきました。従来は天然染料の「藍（あい）」ぞめで、紺色と白の清涼感のあるものが主流でした。

最近は、赤、黄、オレンジ、ピンク、グリーン、紫といった大胆な色使いで、柄も伝統的なもの、たとえば花柄でも**アサガオ**や**アヤメ**などに代わって、**ラン**や**ハイビスカス**などの洋風のものが好まれ、よく売れているといいます。

以前は浴衣といえば生地を買って自分で、あるいは母や祖母に縫ってもらうのが普通でした。最近は浴衣を縫える人が減って、「仕立て上がり」のものを買い求める人が多くなっていますが、仕立職人の不足で、生産が注

reflecting changing practices in Japanese clothing habits over the past few decades, and more particularly the increasing adoption of Western dress. But this trend saw a slight reversal during the 1990s, when *yukata* came to be looked on in a new light, and young women in particular came to see it as an exotic kind of summer fashion. It has consequently enjoyed something of a quiet boom. At fireworks, or summer parties, it's quite chic to go out wearing a *yukata.*

The designs and **color schemes** of *yukata* have changed in keeping with the changing tastes of young people. In the past, *yukata* were typically a cool combination of dark indigo blue and white.

Nowadays *yukata* makers make bold use of vibrant colors like red, yellow, orange, pink, green and purple. The patterns on the *yukata* have likewise changed. In the past, typical Japanese flowers like **morning glories** and **irises** formed the standard motifs; nowadays young people prefer Western flowers like **orchids** and **hibiscus**, and *yukata* with these kinds of patterns sell well.

In the past a girl would usually buy a bolt of the material and sew the *yukata* herself, or rely on her mother or grandmother to do so. Nowadays there are few people who can sew their own *yukata*, and most people buy the garments made by professionals. Apparently, however, the shortage of tailors and seamstresses has led

文に間に合わないほどだといいます。

　お値段はだいたい1着2、3万円、帯や下駄、ハンドバッグ代わりに持つ袋物などの小物まで一式揃えると、4、5万円かかりますが、若者たちは普段着ているTシャツやGパンとはがらっと変わった雰囲気を楽しんでいるようです。

相撲力士・歌舞伎役者も浴衣を着る

　浴衣はまた、歌舞伎などの役者の楽屋着、あるいは相撲の力士の**普段着**として使われています。お中元の時期などに、特別に注文した芸名やしこ名を染め抜いた**反物**を、**ごひいき筋**や有力な後援者などに配って、日ごろの引き立てに感謝する習わしもあります。

　日本の夏はこれからが本番、夏祭りや花火大会など浴衣姿の映える催しが日本各地で賑やかに行われます。

　日本ひとくち歳時記、今日は「浴衣」についてお話ししました。

to demand outstripping production.

A *yukata* usually costs from 20,000 to 30,000 yen, and when the silk sash, *geta* sandals, as well as accessories such as a pouch bag are added in, the whole ensemble can cost up to 40,000 or 50,000 yen. Nevertheless, many young women enjoy the experience of changing out of their daily outfits of T-shirts and **jeans** into this classier alternative.

Many *kabuki* actors like to wear *yukata* when offstage, and *sumō* wrestlers habitually wear them as **daily clothing**. At the time of the summer gift-giving season, performers and wrestlers frequently make gifts to their major **patrons** and backers of **bolts of cloth** dyed with their professional names, to demonstrate their appreciation for their steady patronage and support.

The height of Japan's summer is now just upon us, and soon there will be all sorts of events—summer festivals, evening firework displays throughout Japan—in which all varieties of *yukata* will be seen.

This has been *Around the Year in Japan*. On today's program we discussed *yukata*, the informal summer kimono.

浴衣 ゆかた
1: 木綿の単（ひとえ）長着。夏、または入浴後に着る。高級物には綿縮み・綿絽（ろ）などがある。湯あがり。2:「ゆかたびら」の略。

秋 | Autumn

Part 3

地　震
Earthquakes

日本ひとくち歳時記、今日は「地震」について
お話ししましょう。

This is *Around the Year in Japan*. Today we are
going to talk about earthquakes.

9月1日が防災の日になった理由

9月1日は日本では**防災の日**とされています。なぜ9月1日かというと、この日があの関東大震災が起きた日だからです。

1923年9月1日の正午直前、マグニチュード7.9の大地震が関東地方を襲いました。ちょうど昼食の支度の時間に当たっていたため、台所の火などから大火事が発生し、14万2000人もの**死者、行方不明者**を出す大災害になってしまいました。

これを教訓として、政府は1960年に9月1日を防災の日と制定しました。

とにかく日本は地震が大変多い国です。天井から吊るした電灯がユラユラ揺れるくらいは日常茶飯事、飾り棚の人形が倒れるくらいなら驚く

It's only a small earthquake!

September 1 is designated as **Disaster Prevention Day** in Japan. Why this particular day? Because September 1 was the day in 1923 that the Great Kantō Earthquake occurred.

On September 1, 1923, just before noon, a tremendous earthquake of magnitude 7.9 struck the Greater Tōkyō region. It occurred just as midday meals were being cooked, so fires spread quickly from kitchens to become great conflagrations, resulting in a natural disaster of huge proportions, with a total of 142,000 **fatalities** and **people unaccounted for**.

It was in commemoration of this great tragedy that in 1960 the Japanese government established September 1 as Disaster Prevention Day.

As you may know, Japan is a country where earthquakes are extremely frequent. Japanese are quite accustomed to seeing ceiling light fixtures suddenly start to swing and sway, and nobody is particularly surprised

ほどではありません。なにしろここ130年に限ってみても、日本では、100人以上の犠牲者を出す大地震が19回起きているのです。これは平均すると約6年半に1回という計算になります。

ではなぜ日本ではこんなに地震が多いのでしょうか。

日本はどうしてこんなに地震が多い?

地震の原因としては、**火山活動**によるもの、**断層**、つまり、地層にできた裂け目が動くことによって起きるもの、さらにプレートと呼ばれる地底深くの**巨大な岩盤**の動きによって起きるものなどがありますが、日本列島はちょうどいくつかのプレートがぶつかりあう上に乗っているうえに、**火山帯と断層帯**が数多く走っているため、日本周辺は世界の地震の1割が発生するといわれるほど地震の多発地帯になっています。

それだけに日本では地震に関する研究はたいへん盛んです。**気象庁**が開発した地震活動の総合監視システムは全国の観測地点からのデータを解析して予知情報を作成しています。また専門家で構成する**地震予知連絡会**が設けられていて、定期的に会合

when a tremor brings ornaments on shelves tumbling down. In the last 130 years alone there have been 19 earthquakes that have taken more than one hundred lives. This translates into a killer earthquake about once every six and a half years.

But why is Japan so prone to earthquakes?

Earthquakes arise because of **volcanic activity**, the shifting of **faults**, that is to say cracks in the upper layers of the earth's crust, and the movements of **gigantic slabs** or plates deep within the earth. Japan happens to be located exactly where several of these plates come together and press against each other, and furthermore it is criss-crossed with numerous **volcanic zones and faults**. Because of these elements, about one-tenth of all the world's earthquakes are estimated to occur in the Japanese archipelago.

This also explains why there is a good deal of earth-quake research in Japan. A fully coordinated earthquake surveillance system developed by the **Japan Meteorological Agency** employs and collates seismic observation data from around the country in order to try to predict the occurrence of tremors. Earthquake experts, or seismologists, have formed a **Coordinating Committee for Earthquake Prediction** to

を開き情報の分析を行っています。

地震は予知以上に
防災対策がたいせつ

　しかしそれにもかかわらず、6000人以上の犠牲者を出した**阪神大震災**を的確に予知して対策を立てることはできませんでした。個々の地震を的確に予知するのは、まだまだ困難だというのが実情です。

　そうなると、とりわけ重要なのが防災対策で、阪神大震災の後、防災施設を拡充整備するための法律が新たに**制定され**、5ヵ年計画が立てられました。また市民の防災意識も高まり、**耐震建築の家屋**が人気を集め、防災用品を購入する人も増えています。タンスや本棚を壁に固定する器具や窓ガラスの飛散を防ぐフィルム、**防災頭巾**、水をためておくための**ポリタンク**、また、**懐中電灯**や携帯ラジオ、薬品、着替え、缶詰などをリュックに詰めた防災セットなどがよく売れています。

　日本ひとくち歳時記、今日は「地震」についてお話ししました。

bring their collective expertise to bear on the problem, holding regular meetings and sharing their research findings.

Despite these efforts, no one was able to predict the **Great Hanshin Earthquake** that struck the Kōbe area, taking the lives of more than 6,000 people. The fact is that accurate prediction of individual earthquakes is still very difficult.

This means that it is extremely important to be prepared to respond to these disasters. After the Kōbe earthquake, a new law was **enacted** for the expansion within five years of various facilities in the event of an earthquake. As the general public becomes increasingly aware of the importance of being aware of earthquake disaster prevention, **earthquake-proof housing** has become popular, and more and more people are buying items designed for use in the event of an earthquake. These include fixtures to secure cabinets, bookshelves and other furniture to walls, protective film to prevent window glass from shattering, **protective headgear**, and **polyethylene tanks** to collect water. Rucksacks prepacked with equipment vital in the event of an earthquake or any other natural disaster, including **flashlights**, portable radio, medicine, a change of clothes, and canned food, are also selling well.

This has been *Around the Year in Japan*. On today's program we discussed earthquakes.

台　風
Typhoons

日本ひとくち歳時記、今日は「台風」について
お話ししましょう。

This is *Around the Year in Japan*. Today we are
going to talk about typhoons.

**台風は地震と並ぶ
大きな自然災害**

地震と並んで、日本に大きな災害をもたらすもう一つの自然現象が台風です。

　台風は、北太平洋西部の熱帯の海上で発生して、日本列島やフィリピン諸島、アジア大陸東南部などを襲う**熱帯性低気圧**のうち、**最大風速**が毎秒17メートル以上に達したものをいいます。6月から12月を中心に、毎年20個から40個発生。このうち10個ぐらいが日本に近づき、3個ぐらいが上陸します。

　台風が日本を襲う7月から9月にかけては農作物が花をつけたり、実をつける時期に当たるため、農家は昔からこの台風を恐れてきました。日

B esides earthquakes, Japan has another principle cause of natural disasters, and this is typhoons.

Typhoons are **tropical low pressure systems** that are spawned above the warm waters in the western part of the North Pacific, and then move northward to crash into the Japanese archipelago, the Philippine Islands, the southeastern edge of the Asian continent, and other areas. **Maximum wind speed** has to exceed 17 meters per second for them to be defined as a typhoon. Typhoons occur primarily between June and December, generally numbering 20 to 40 a year. On average, approximately 10 of these approach the shores of Japan and about 3 of these actually come inland.

Most of the typhoons hit Japan between the months of July and September, just when crops are flowering or ripening, so from ancient times typhoons have been dreaded by farmers. If strong typhoons hit the rice crop

本の農業の中心的な作物である稲の開花期に、強い雨風で**受粉**できなかったり、稲が倒れたり、あるいは田畑が水をかぶってしまうと、当然収穫が落ちてしまいます。

また果樹でも、リンゴ、ナシ、ブドウなどがこれから実が熟していくという時期に台風に当たると、被害も大きなものとなります。数年前、リンゴの主産地の一つ青森県で、台風のためにほとんどのリンゴが一夜にして落ちてしまい、大きな被害を受けました。

また、別の台風では、日本家屋の重要な材料である**杉**の産地として有名な大分県で、いくつもの山の杉の木がなぎたおされてしまい、これも大きな被害をもたらしました。

台風による洪水、高潮などの被害は甚大

それにも増して恐ろしいのが、大雨、強風によって起きる**洪水、崖崩れ**などです。大雨で増水した河川の氾濫で水浸しになるだけではありません。日本の地形は山が多く、**住宅**が急傾斜の土地に作られることが多いため、土砂崩れで家が押しつぶされたり、流されてしまうことが珍しくないのです。

just at the time the seedlings are coming into bud, and prevent the seedlings from **pollinating**, or knock the ears of grain flat, or inundate the rice paddies, naturally the harvest will be reduced.

Fruit trees, such as apple and pear, and grape vines, which are ripening during this period, can also suffer tremendous damage. Several years ago, Aomori Prefecture in northern Japan, one of the country's principal apple production areas, was so devastated by a major typhoon that all the apples were knocked off the trees in a single night, wiping out the crop with huge financial losses.

Similarly, another giant typhoon hit Ōita Prefecture, a leading production center of **cedar**, one of the most important materials used in the construction of Japanese style wooden homes. It cut giant swathes through the hills, uprooting hundreds of trees and causing great damage.

Even more terrifying than the typhoon itself can be the damage caused by the **floods**, **landslides** and mudslides that can result from the heavy rains and strong winds that are a typhoon's principal characteristics. Rivers swollen by heavy rains may overflow their banks and inundate the surrounding land. Because Japan is so mountainous, many **dwellings** are built on steep slopes, and it is by no means rare for them to be crushed or swept away.

また、海岸地方では高潮による被害も起きます。1959年に本州の中央部を横断した伊勢湾台風では、死者行方不明者5100人という大変な被害を出しましたが、そのうちの70パーセント以上は高潮によるものでした。

この「高潮」というのは、気圧が異常に低くなることによって海面が持ち上げられ、さらに強い風によって海水が吹き寄せられ、海岸の海面が異常に高くなる現象です。

台風はマイナスだけでなくプラス面もある

しかし、台風はこうしたマイナスの面だけを持っているわけではありません。それは、国土に大量の水をもたらしてくれるという側面です。一つの台風が日本全体に降らす雨量は、50億トンから450億トン。

中には1976年の台風17号のように、日本近海に長く留まって800億トンもの雨を降らせたものもありました。夏から秋にかけての台風は、冬の降雪、初夏の梅雨と並んで、日本の3大水源ともいわれているのです。

先ほどの伊勢湾台風をはじめ、何千人もの死者行方不明者が出る台風が、以前はいくつもありました。しかし現在では、台風が襲来しても、人命が大

High tides in **coastal areas** can also wreak heavy damage. The huge typhoon now known as the "Ise Bay Typhoon," which swept across central Japan in 1959, left an enormous number of people (5,100) dead or unaccounted for. More than 70 percent of these were victims of high tides.

These high tides are generated when unusually low air pressure causes the surface of the ocean to rise, and the high winds make the ocean water pile up, so that the water level in the affected coastal areas becomes abnormally high.

The effects of typhoons aren't all negative. For one thing, they bring with them huge amounts of fresh water. A single typhoon, it is estimated, can bring Japan between 5 billion and 45 billion tons.

Typhoon Number 17 in 1976 brought an incredible 80 billion tons, since it stayed for a long time and rain fell continuously. The typhoons in summer and autumn, together with the rain and snow in winter and the rainfall of the early summer rainy season constitute Japan's three most important sources of fresh water.

There have been several typhoons in recorded history that have killed or left missing several thousand people, including the previously mentioned Ise Bay Typhoon. Nowadays, when such huge storms slam into heavily

量に失われることはなくなってきています。理由としては、河川の堤防や防潮堤の整備などの防災対策が進められたことがあげられます。

**きめ細かに行われる
台風の観測態勢**

　もう一つ忘れてならないのが、気象観測態勢の充実と、報道機関による周知でしょう。**気象衛星**によって台風発生の初期の段階から追跡できるようになった他、台風が日本に近付くと、全国に設置されたレーダーで雲や雨の様子、動きが細かく観測され、注意報、警報がきめ細かに出されます。さらに、その情報がテレビ・ラジオを通じて流され、**余裕**を持って対策をとれるようになったのです。

　日本ひとくち歳時記、今日は「台風」についてお話ししました。

populated areas, not so many lives are lost. This is because disaster measures have been taken: rivers have been provided with embankments, and dikes and coastal barriers reinforced.

Another factor that should not be forgotten is the increasing sophistication of weather forecasts, and the role of the mass media in getting information out to the public. **Weather satellites** track typhoons from soon after they are spawned, and as a typhoon nears Japan, numerous radar sites throughout the nation keep a sharp watch on cloud and rain conditions, and severe storm warnings are issued. These are broadcast on both TV and radio, which gives everybody considerable **leeway** to respond to the threats posed by typhoons.

This has been *Around the Year in Japan*. On today's program we discussed typhoons.

台風
北西太平洋の低緯度域に発生する熱帯低気圧のうち、中心付近の最大風速が毎秒17m以上に達したもの。日本には8〜9月に多く襲来し、大きな被害をもたらす。タイフーン。typhoon。

運動会
Athletic Meets

日本ひとくち歳時記、今日は「運動会」について
お話ししましょう。

This is *Around the Year in Japan*. Today we are
going to talk about the Japanese custom of holding
undōkai, or "athletic meets."

**職場でも行われる
日本の運動会**

運動会というのは普通、幼稚園から小、中、高校の単位で、全員が参加して行われるスポーツ大会をさします。

スポーツを楽しむと同時に**親睦**を深める目的で、企業や職場、地域単位で開かれることもあります。運動会が、取引先や家族を招待して催す、会社の恒例の行事になっているような場合もあります。

なぜこの季節（10月）に運動会かというと、9月中は台風が来て、なかなかお天気が安定しませんが、それが過ぎると秋晴れの日が続くことが多いというのが一番の理由でしょう。

9月に**2学期**が始まるとまもなく、日

Usually when we refer to athletic meets, we mean the sports days that are held for the whole school at kindergartens and primary, junior high and high schools.

There is also another kind of athletic meet that companies, offices and local neighborhoods sometimes hold, with the dual purpose of giving people the opportunity to enjoy sports and enhancing **camaraderie**. In some companies, athletic meets have become regular company functions, with company clients and workers' families invited to attend.

To understand why athletic meets are held at this particular time of year (October), one has to remember the weather conditions in Japan. September is usually a month in which typhoons occur, which means that the weather is usually quite unstable, but after that period there follow many days of continuously fine autumn weather, highly suitable for athletic meets.

Soon after the **second semester** of the Japanese

本全国の学校で、子供たちが運動会の出し物や**応援**の練習をする風景が見られ、号令やホイッスル、行進曲や太鼓の音が聞こえてくるようになります。

運動会本番は家族が見に来ることのできる週末、たいてい日曜日に行われます。生徒たちは紅白の二組に分かれて得点を競います。どちらの組に属しているかは、帽子か額に結んだはちまきの色で区別できます。

種目は**徒競走**やリレー、**障害物競走**、低学年の生徒の遊技やダンス、高学年の生徒の組体操や騎馬戦、教師や父母の参加するゲームや競技などもあって盛りだくさんです。応援団の打ち鳴らす大太鼓にあわせて、拍手や声援を送る応援合戦も見所の一つです。

朝から夕方まで**1日がかりの行事**ですから、昼食は応援に来た家族といっしょにとることが多く、昼休みに校庭のあちこちに敷物を敷いてお弁当を広げるのが運動会の楽しみの一つにもなっています。

写真やビデオにわが子の活躍ぶり

運動会で行われる主要な種目は？

school year begins in September, we see children at schools throughout the country practicing for the events and rehearsing their **cheering** routines. We also hear the words of encouragement and orders barked by coaches, and whistles, marching songs and beating drums.

The actual athletic meets themselves are held on weekends, usually on a Sunday, so that families can attend. The children are divided into two teams, the "red" and the "white" team, which compete against each other for points. Children belonging to each team wear either a red or a white cap or a *hachimaki* headband.

The events include **footraces**, relays, **obstacle races**, and, for lower grade students, games and dancing. The older students perform group exercises, or play team games and contests such as *kibasen*, or the cavalry battle. There are also games and competitive events for the teachers and parents to participate in. It's a sight in itself to see the supporters of the two sides clapping and shouting along with the pounding of the drums.

An athletic meet is an **all-day event** lasting from early morning till late afternoon, so most students eat lunch with family members who've come to cheer them on. One of the most enjoyable aspects of an athletic meet is spreading out a mat somewhere in the grounds of the school during lunchtime and sitting down to enjoy a box lunch.

You often see mothers and fathers taking the event

を撮っておこうと、子供たち以上に張り切っている父母の姿も見かけられます。

ところで、運動会が日本で始まったのは、19世紀後半、**明治維新後**のことです。1872年に近代的な学校制度が発足し、外国から招かれた教師が、あらゆる教科の指導に当たりましたが、運動会も外国人教師のいた学校から始まり、やがて**小学校**で広く行われるようになりました。

明治維新後に始まった日本の運動会

とはいっても当時はまだ学校のグラウンドなども十分整備されていなかったので、河原や海岸、神社の境内（けいだい）などに出かけて、体操をしたり、**綱引き**や**旗取り**などの伝統的な遊びに興じたといいます。

1910年代以降になるとグラウンド整備も進み、校庭運動会が主流になります。競技の方も集団訓練的なものより、娯楽性の高い出し物に人気が集まり、万国旗で飾られた校庭の周りには**屋台**や**模擬店**が並び、**花火**が上がり、仮装行列や地域対抗**リレー**で盛り上がるといったふうに町ぐるみ、村ぐるみのレクリエーションという色彩が強まりました。

much more seriously than their children, recording the events and achievements of their offspring with cameras and video equipment.

The tradition of *undōkai* started during the latter half of the 19th century, after the **Meiji Restoration**. In 1872 the modern educational system was launched and foreign teachers were invited to Japan to provide instruction in all sorts of subjects. Athletic meets were first held at schools with foreign instructors, and then later spread widely at the **primary school** level.

Even so, in those days school grounds were hardly suitable for sports events, so they were staged on riverbanks, beaches, shrine grounds, or other open areas, with gymnastics and other more traditional games, such as **tugs-of-war** and **flag races**.

From the 1910s school grounds became more adequately equipped, and athletic meets came to be held there. Competitive events that were fun both to participate in and to watch came to be valued more than events that emphasized group discipline and coordination. **Food stalls** and **refreshment booths** made their appearance alongside the schoolyards decked out with flags from around the world, and there were also **firework displays**. Lively events such as fancy dress parades and **relay races** held between different villages gave the

　学齢期の子供の数が減り、さまざまな娯楽を個人個人が楽しむようになった現在、運動会の意味は、特に都会では薄れつつあるようです。しかし運動会は1970年代ごろまで、学校の枠を越えて人々に親しまれる地域の大イベントだったのです。

　日本ひとくち歳時記、今日は「運動会」についてお話ししました。

events a very community-oriented flavor.

Nowadays, with the number of school age children on the decline and all sorts of games and recreation available for enjoyment on an individual basis, athletic meets have lost some of the aura they once had, especially in urban areas. Nevertheless, up until around the 1970s, they were events that transcended the framework of the school itself and were loved by the entire community.

This has been *Around the Year in Japan*. On today's program we discussed *undōkai*, or "athletic meets."

運動会
学校・会社・団体などで、各種の運動競技・遊戯を競い合い、楽しみ合う会。athletic meet。

米
Rice

日本ひとくち歳時記、今日は「米」について
お話ししましょう。

This is *Around the Year in Japan*. Today we are
going to talk about rice.

**新米のおいしさは
格別のものがある**

秋、日本の農村は、**黄金色の稲穂**が青い空に映えて美しい実りの季節を迎えます。稲の刈り入れは気温の低い北海道や東北地方では9月に始まり、徐々に南下し、最も暖かい九州、沖縄などでは11月に収穫期となります。それとともに、各地の米屋やスーパーの店先に、「新米」と書かれた米袋が目に付くようになります。

日本では収穫して1年以内の米を特に「新米」と呼びます。米を**主食**とする地域の方々はよくご存知のように、米は収穫の数年後でも**保存状態**さえ良ければ十分に食べられますが、その年とれたての新米が何といっても一番おいしいのです。**水分**を多く含んでいて、ふっくらと炊け、舌触りも香りも良いからです。

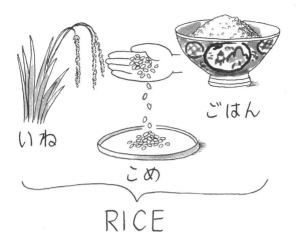

いね　ごはん　こめ

RICE

Autumn is a beautiful season in rural communities in Japan: it's harvest time, when the **golden ears of rice** wave against a background of clear blue skies. Harvest time begins in September in the cooler areas of the country, such as Hokkaidō and Tōhoku. In the warmer regions, like Kyūshū and Okinawa, it begins in November. At this time, all around the country sacks with tags saying "New Rice" are displayed prominently in rice shops and supermarkets.

The term "New Rice" applies specifically to rice harvested within the past year. As those of our listeners from countries where rice is the **staple food** know, rice grain can actually be stored for several years, providing **storage conditions** are good, before being consumed. Nevertheless, "New Rice" does have an especially delicious flavor. It has a high **moisture** content, so it cooks well, becoming soft and fluffy, and it has a wonderful taste and fragrance.

米の味は品種ごとに千差万別

米の味は、また、稲の品種によっても差があります。日本で栽培されている稲の品種は数百種に上り、それぞれに名前がついています。たとえばコシヒカリ、ヒノヒカリ、など「光」という字がついたもの、ササニシキ、キヨニシキ、など「錦」という字がついたもの、そのほか、「日本晴」「ひとめぼれ」「あきたこまち」などといったイメージの良い名前がつけられています。

このうち一番人気はコシヒカリで、米所新潟県産のコシヒカリは平均の値段の2倍近くの値で売られています。

米不足で起こった"大パニック"

ところで、長らく米を主食にしてきて米の味にはちょっとうるさい日本人が、数年前、大パニックに襲われる事件がありました。1993年の秋は米が凶作で、国内で消費する量をまかなえず、外国からの輸入に頼らざるをえない事態になったのです。日本人は普段、炊いたとき粘りのあるジャポニカ種の米を食べ慣れていますが、輸入米の中にはパサパサした舌触りのインディカ種の米もあり、買ったものの口に合わないと捨ててしまう

Different varieties of rice vary in taste. There are several hundred varieties of rice in Japan, and they all have their own names. *Koshihikari*, *Hinohikari* and some other varieties include the word *hikari*, which means "shining" or "gleaming." *Sasanishiki* and *Kiyonishiki* include the word *nishiki*, which means "brocade." Among other representative names are *Nihonbare* ("Clear Sky"), *Hitomebore* ("Love at First Sight") and *Akita komachi* ("Akita Beauty"). They are all meant to evoke an appealing association.

The strain of rice most highly favored is *Koshihikari*, and the most sought after of all *Koshihikari* rice is that produced in Niigata Prefecture on the Japan Sea side of Japan. *Koshihikari* rice grown here sells for nearly twice the price of ordinary rice.

Japanese people can be somewhat **finicky** about their rice, since, after all, it has been their staple food a very long time. This was proved several years ago when a huge panic resulted from the sudden decrease in rice supplies due to a poor harvest in the autumn of 1993, and large amounts of rice had to be imported. The variety of rice Japanese are accustomed to eating is the *Japonica* variety, which fluffs up and becomes sticky after being boiled. Among the varieties that were imported at that time were **Indica types**, rather too dry for Japanese taste. A lot of the imported rice ended up being discarded, which brought the Japanese in for some criticism.

人まで出て物議をかもしました。この時期、米食を減らしてパンや麺類にしたという人も少なくありません。

じつは、日本人の米の消費量はこのところ減り続けています。これまでで米の消費量が最大だった1962年には国民1人当たり118キロの米を消費していたのが、1996年には66キロにまで減少しています。一月当たりにすると1人が10キロ食べていたのが5・5キロになったわけですから、約半分に減っています。

また、最近の調査では、1日3食のうち3食とも米を食べている人は全体の13パーセントで、2食が米という人が60パーセント、米のご飯は1日1食だけという人が26パーセントでした。米のご飯はぜんぜん食べないという人は1パーセントにも達していませんから、まだまだ主食としての米の座は揺るぎないものの、若い女性や子供たちの間に「米離れ」が著しいところをみると、米の消費量は今後も回復しそうにありません。

日本ひとくち歳時記、今日は「米」についてお話ししました。

減少し続ける日本人の米の消費量

At the time quite a number of people cut down on their consumption of rice and turned to bread and noodles instead.

In point of fact, the amount of rice consumed by Japanese has continued to decline over the years. In 1962, when **rice consumption** was at its peak, per capita annual consumption for the Japanese was 118 kilograms. By 1996 it had plummeted to 66 kilograms. This works out to a decrease of nearly 50 percent in average monthly consumption, from about 10 kilograms to about 5.5 kilograms.

Recent surveys show that only 13 percent of those polled eat rice regularly at all three meals. Sixty percent eat it at two meals, and 26 percent at one. Less than 1 percent of respondents said they didn't eat rice at all, so rice still reigns as the staple food of choice for the Japanese. Nevertheless, a significant number of young women and children are turning away from rice, a fact which makes it unlikely that rice consumption will show any significant rebound in the future.

This has been *Around the Year in Japan*. On today's program we discussed rice.

紅葉狩り
Viewing Autumn Foliage

日本ひとくち歳時記、今日は「紅葉狩り」について
お話ししましょう。

This is *Around the Year in Japan*. Today we are
going to talk about *momiji-gari*, or "viewing
autumn foliage."

日本人が桜の季節に「花見」を
楽しむことはよく知られていま
すが、日本人はまた、野山の紅葉を
日本の秋の典型的な美と考え、これ
を見に出かけることを「紅葉狩り」と
呼んでいます。「紅葉狩り」は、花見
と並ぶ代表的な季節行事として、日
本人の生活に深く根ざしているので
す。

　「紅葉狩り」は、「花見」同様、日
本で最も古い歌集、『万葉集』にすで
にうたわれています。7世紀の人で
『万葉集』の代表的な歌人、柿本人麻
呂は「春へには花かざし持ち、秋立
てば紅葉かざせり」と詠んでいます
が、初めはもっぱら宮廷や貴族の優

That the Japanese people delight in flower viewing, when the **cherry blossoms** appear in spring, is well known. But they also regard the season of autumn as the height of beauty, and the red and yellow autumn foliage as one of the particular beauties of the season. The pleasurable pastime of viewing autumn colors is called *momiji-gari*, which literally means "hunting the autumn leaves." Japanese people enjoy *momiji-gari*, which is regarded as a seasonal event equally as important as *hanami*, or flower viewing, and both practices are deeply rooted in the lives of the Japanese.

Just as with *hanami*, this term can be found in the *Manyōshu* (*Collection of Ten Thousand Leaves*), Japan's oldest collection of poetry. One of the main contributors to that collection, Kakinomoto Hitomaro, wrote a poem in the 7th century describing sprays of decorative blossoms in spring and swathes of coppery autumn leaves. The practice of viewing autumn colors is thought to

雅な遊びだったようです。

　それが17世紀ごろ、江戸時代に入ってから庶民の間に広まり、紅葉を見ながら酒盛りをしたり、**趣向を凝らした食事**を楽しんだりするようになりました。

　日本は南北に細長く広がる**列島**ですから、北の北海道では9月の末ごろから紅葉が始まり、だんだん南の地方へと広がってゆきます。また日本は国土の70パーセント以上が山地ですから、都市の近郊でも山寄りの所は紅葉が早く楽しめるようになります。

**紅葉は9月末から
徐々に全国に広がる**

　この季節になると、毎日のようにテレビ画面を紅葉の名所の風景が飾り、いつごろ、どこが見ごろになるか報道されます。週末や休日には、特に多くの観光客が「紅葉狩り」に出かけます。

　ところで、「もみじ」というのは、**カエデ、カシワ、ハゼ**、ウルシ、サクラ、**クヌギ、イチョウ**などの**落葉樹**の葉が、赤や黄色に変わることをさすのですが、中でも特にカエデの葉が見事に紅葉するところから、カエデの別称として「もみじ」が用いられることもありま

have started off as an elegant pastime mainly enjoyed by the court and **aristocracy**.

That changed, however, around the 17th Century, during the Edo period (1600–1868), when the custom spread to commoners, and people began to hold *sake* parties and **sumptuous feasts** while viewing the beautiful autumn landscapes.

Japan consists of a long **archipelago**, and the leaves begin to turn in Hokkaidō as early as late September. The change in the color of the leaves gradually moves southward down the islands, much like a weather front. Many favorite spots for *momiji-gari* are within relatively easy access of even major urban centers, since 70 percent of Japan is mountains.

With the arrival of the autumn season, TV programs feature spots especially famous for their autumn foliage nearly every day, with detailed information on when and where to enjoy the most beautiful sights. On weekends and holidays, droves of people set out eager to see the autumn colors.

The use of the term *momiji* is quite interesting in this connection. In general it is applied to all **deciduous trees** that produce autumnal leaves tinged with a red or yellow color, including **maple**, **oak**, **sumac**, the Japanese lacquer tree, cherry, the *kunugi* oak and the **ginkgo**. But it has also come to be used to denote the maple, the actual name for which is *kaede*, because of the particular

す。また、木の葉ではなく、山野の雑草の紅葉を「草もみじ」と呼び、これもまた風情のあるものと見ます。

桜が花の盛りに雨や風で、はかなく散ってしまうように、紅葉の錦にたとえられる華やかさも、変わりやすくもろく散ってしまいます。この辺が日本人の心にぴったりくるのでしょう。

紅葉、そして「紅葉狩り」は短歌や俳句に飽かずに詠まれ、**屏風絵**や浮世絵に繰り返し描かれ、着物や帯の伝統的な模様のモチーフとして親しまれ、能や歌舞伎の題材ともなりました。

伝説に基づく能の「紅葉狩」とは?

紅葉にまつわる伝説に基づく、能の「紅葉狩」をご紹介しましょう。

ある貴人が信濃の国で**鹿狩り**に行く途中、紅葉狩りの酒宴へ向かう貴婦人たちに出会います。見慣れぬ貴婦人たちは訝る貴人を引き留め、酒を勧めて美しく舞い踊ります。

酔い伏した貴人の所に八幡宮の使者が現れて、女たちは戸隠山の鬼神

beauty of the leaves of that tree. The term *kusa momiji* is similarly used to describe the autumn colors of the various grasses that cover the hills in autumn.

Just as cherry blossoms scatter in the wind or rain when right at their prime, the golden and red leaves of autumn, often compared to brocade, can swiftly lose their color and fall. This evanescence appeals perfectly to the Japanese sensibility.

The Japanese people never tire of reciting *tanka* or *haiku* poems about the autumn foliage and the joys of viewing it. **Folding screen** paintings, *ukiyo-e* woodblock prints and other art forms frequently seek to portray the splendor of autumn, and kimono and *obi* sashes or kimonos half made of silk have also incorporated special traditional autumn motifs. The *momiji* tradition has also found expression in the *noh* and *kabuki* theatrical forms.

Here is a brief summary of the *noh* play entitled *Momiji-gari*.

One day a certain aristocrat sets out to hunt for **deer** in the mountainous province of Shinano (now in Nagano Prefecture), when he comes upon some court ladies enjoying a *sake* party while viewing the autumn leaves. They invite him to join them, though he has never seen them before, pour him cups of *sake*, and perform a graceful dance.

As the gentleman dozes off tipsily, suddenly a messenger from the *Hachimangu* Shrine appears and tells him

であると告げ、神剣を与えます。目覚めた貴人に鬼が襲いかかりますが、貴人は神剣を使って闘い、鬼は退治されて舞台は終わります。

　燃え上がるような紅葉の、非日常的な美しさが、満開の桜と同じように日本人の美意識や想像力を刺激して、伝説や戯曲を生み出す霊感の源泉となるのかもしれません。

　日本ひとくち歳時記、今日は「紅葉狩り」についてお話ししました。

that the women are actually demons from a nearby mountain, Togakushi, and gives him a sacred sword for protection. The aristocrat, now fully awake, is then attacked by the demons, but he is able to vanquish them with the help of the divine sword, and thus the play ends.

The extraordinary beauty of the blazing autumn foliage has, like the cherry blossoms at their height, served to stimulate both the Japanese sense of beauty and imagination. Both became wellsprings for legends and plays.

This has been *Around the Year in Japan*. On today's program we discussed *momiji-gari*, or "viewing autumn foliage."

紅葉狩 [り]

1: 山野に出て紅葉を鑑賞すること。古代から平安時代にかけて花見とともに広く行われた行楽。2:《紅葉狩り》①謡曲の曲名。五番目物(切(きり)能物)。観世信光(かんぜのぶみつ)作。戸隠(とがくし)山で、上臈(じょうろう)姿の鬼女が本性を現して平維茂(たいらのこれもち)を襲うが逆に討たれる。②新歌舞伎(かぶき)十八番の一つ。謡曲『紅葉狩』による歌舞伎舞踊。③長唄(ながうた)・荻江節(おぎえぶし)・地唄(じうた)・一中節(いっちゅうぶし)などの曲名。

七五三
The Seven-Five-Three Festival

日本ひとくち歳時記、今日は秋の子供のお祝い、「七五三」についてお話ししましょう。

This is *Around the Year in Japan*. Today we are going to talk about the *Shichigosan* festival for children.

七五三の神社は晴れ着の子供で一杯

11月15日、日本全国の神社は、晴れ着で着飾った子供たちで賑わいます。七五三のお祝いです。その名のとおり、7歳の女の子、5歳の男の子、3歳の男女の子供のためのお祝いです。

振り袖姿の女の子や**蝶ネクタイ**をした男の子など、いつものやんちゃぶりはどこへやら、**神妙な**顔つきで神社に向かいます。

子供たちの父母はもちろん、中にはおじいちゃん、おばあちゃんもいっしょという家族もいます。そして、神殿で神官の**お払い**を受け、健やかな成長を願うのです。

このNHKのすぐそばにある、大き

やっぱり 3つの時の
着物じゃ ダメね

On November 15 at **Shinto shrines** throughout Japan we see throngs of gorgeously decked out children, who are celebrating the *Shichigosan* (Seven-Five-Three) Festival. As the name suggests, this is a festival for children aged seven, five and three—more specifically, girls of seven, boys of five, and boys and girls three years in age.

The girls wear long-sleeved kimono, and the boys suits and **bow ties**. Usually they are little tearaways and ruffians, but that seems to disappear on this special day, and they head toward the shrines with **solemn** expressions on their faces.

With the children inevitably come their parents, and in many cases their grandparents as well. In front of the shrine, the children go through an act of **ceremonial purification** conducted by a Shinto priest, who prays that they will grow up to be healthy and strong.

Quite near NHK headquarters here in Tōkyō is Meiji

な神社、明治神宮もそうした親子連れが大勢訪れます。子供たちは揃って、長い紙の袋を下げています。中には直径1センチ半、長さ30センチほどの白く長い飴が何本も入っています。これを千歳飴といいます。この飴をなめれば、1000年の長寿を保つことができるという意味です。

七五三は公家や武家の風習として誕生

さかのぼると、このお祝いは、公家や武家の昔の風習が元になっています。むかし、子供たちは生まれてから3歳になるまで、髪の毛を剃っていましたが、3歳を期に髪を伸ばしました。また5歳になると、男の子は礼装である袴を着けるようになりました。そして7歳になった女の子は、それまで着物は簡単なつけ紐で着ていたのを、きちんとした帯で締めるようになりました。

こうした風習が江戸時代に入って、江戸、今の東京の一般の町民の間にも広まったのです。

しかし、七五三という名前でこの祝いが盛んに行われるようになったのは意外に新しく、100年ほど前です。また、第2次大戦の後から広まったという地方もあります。

Jingu, a huge shrine where on this day crowds of parents and children come to celebrate the occasion. The children all carry long paper bags containing sticks of white candy measuring one and a half centimeters in diameter by about 30 centimeters: these are called *Chitose ame*, or Thousand-Year Sweets. Lick this candy, and you will supposedly live a good long life of one thousand years.

The Seven-Five-Three Festival has its origins in the ancient customs of families of the court aristocracy and *samurai*. In olden times, the custom was for children to have their heads shaved from the time they were born till the age of three. Then, their hair was allowed to grow, and from age five boys began to wear *hakama*, a ceremonial pleated skirt. When girls reached the age of seven, they began to tie their kimono with an *obi* of silk or other material; up until that age they tied them with a narrow cord.

These customs and practices caught on with the townsfolk and merchants of the capital of Edo (now Tōkyō) in the Edo period (1600–1868).

But the festival only caught on in a largescale way under the name *Shichigosan* relatively recently, about 100 years ago. In some areas it didn't catch on until after World War II.

七五三が11月15日に行われる理由

では、七五三のお祝いをする11月15日には何か意味があるのでしょうか。稲作が中心の日本の農業では、11月は1年の農作業が終わり、その収穫を祝う時期に当たります。

また、15日は**太陰暦**ではちょうど**満月**、色々な祝日に当てられています。そうしたところから、この日が子供の健やかな成長を祈願する日として選ばれたのではないかといわれています。日本の祝いのそこかしこに現れる稲作。またここにも顔を出していました。

日本ひとくち歳時記、今日は「七五三」についてお話ししました。

But why is the festival held on November 15? Well, for one thing, it's in this month that the annual growing season for rice, the staple crop in Japan, comes to an end, so this is just around the time that people are celebrating having brought in the harvest.

Furthermore, by the **old lunar calendar**, November 15 was the time of the **full moon**. There are, therefore, other holidays in other months of the year also which are designated as festivals and held on the fifteenth. This is apparently the reason that this particular day in November is chosen to pray to the gods for the healthy growth of children. Rice culture makes its presence felt in various ways in the festivals and celebrations of Japan, and this is yet another example.

This has been *Around the Year in Japan*. On today's program we discussed the *Shichigosan* festival for children.

七五三
1: 祝儀に用いるめでたい数。2: 子どもの成長を祝って、男子3歳・5歳、女子3歳・7歳の11月15日に氏神にお参りする行事。七五三の祝い。3: 注連縄 (しめなわ)。4: 本膳 (ほんぜん) が七菜 (七種のおかず)、二の膳が五菜、三の膳が三菜のりっぱな献立。

漬　物
Japanese Pickles

日本ひとくち歳時記、今日は「漬物」について
お話ししましょう。

This is *Around the Year in Japan*. Today we
are going to talk about *tsukemono*, or Japanese
"pickles."

**冬場の保存食として
生まれた漬物**

漬物はもとは食物を貯蔵してお
く保存食として考え出されたも
ので、特に新鮮な野菜などが手に入
りにくくなる冬場の食料として普及
しました。

　ですから世界各地にそれぞれの風
土や気候、食生活などと調和した漬
物があります。日本にもいくつもそん
な漬物があります。

　「ご飯と味噌汁、そしておいしい漬
物があれば他に何もいらない」などと
いう漬物好きは、今や日本人の中で
も少数派になってしまいましたが、そ
れでもスーパーやデパートの食料品売
り場には必ず漬物コーナーがあって、
塩やぬか、味噌や醤油、**酒かす、梅
酢**などに漬けた色とりどりの漬物が

Tsukemono, or "pickles", originally developed from the practice of pickling foodstuffs to preserve them so that they could be eaten over the long winter months, a time when certain foods, especially vegetables, are difficult to grow or obtain.

They are thus various kinds of pickles to be found throughout the world, though the forms they take differ according to local customs, climate and food preferences and taboos. Japan too has its own distinct varieties of pickled foods.

Pickle afficionados will tell you that all you need for a satisfying meal are *miso* ("bean paste") soup, a bowl of rice, and pickles, though nowadays it's probably only a minority who still adhere to this philosophy. But if we walk into any department store or supermarket, we are sure to find a pickle corner in the food section. There we will find vegetables and other foods preserved in salt, **rice bran**, fermented bean paste, soy sauce, *sake* **lees**,

並んでいます。

それも最近は**レトルトパック**などの保存方法の発達で、季節を問わずいつでも、日本各地はもちろん、お隣の韓国製のキムチなどまで食べられるようになりました。

「お茶と漬物で食事を締めくくらないと口がさっぱりしない」という日本人もまだたくさんいて、漬物は日本人にとっていわば「デザート」なのです。

日本の漬物の特徴は、野菜などの材料を使い、塩漬け**発酵**の漬物が多いことです。

材料が野菜主体なのは、仏教伝来以降、肉や魚を使うことを敬遠するようになったためといわれ、それ以前の日本人は、魚や肉類も漬物にして保存していたようです。日本の漬物はまた、概して塩辛いものが多く、白米のご飯によくあいます。

日本の漬物の歴史をたどると、仏教寺院や**僧侶**が大きな役割を果たしてきました。8世紀、奈良時代にはすでに、**ナス**や**瓜**、**カブ**、**桃**などの野菜や果物を塩や酢で漬けたものを僧侶が食用にしていた、という記述が残

日本の漬物の特徴はどこにある？

apricot vinegar and various other preserving substances.

In recent years new methods have been developed, including so-called **retort packs**, to keep food edible, and such modern packaging techniques now allow Japanese to enjoy their favorite pickles from various parts of the country regardless of the season—even *kimchi* from neighboring Korea.

In fact, many Japanese believe that the only way to finish off a meal in a refreshing way is with green tea and pickles. So for some people Japanese pickles are a kind of dessert.

The principal features of Japanese pickles are that they are made from vegetables, and pickled using a process of salting and **fermentation**.

The reason why vegetables are the chief ingredient derives from the fact that eating meat and fish was generally avoided in Japan after Buddhism came to its shores. Before that, the Japanese had apparently partaken of pickled meat or fish. As for the saltiness, this makes the pickles a delicious condiment to go with the bland taste of the white rice which has long been the staple in the Japanese diet.

A look into the history of Japanese pickles shows that Buddhist temples and **priests** have played a significant role. Records survive showing that in the 8th century, during the Nara period, Buddhist priests were already eating pickles made with **eggplants**, **cucumbers**, **turnips**, **peaches** and other vegetables and fruits in salt, vinegar

っています。

　12世紀、鎌倉時代に入ると、さらに洗練された漬物が精進料理に取り入れられ、禅宗寺院などでいちだんと発達することになります。

　著名な禅僧、沢庵和尚が考案したといわれる、干した大根を塩とぬかで漬け込む「沢庵漬け」などがその代表です。

　もう少し時代が下ると、味噌、酒、みりん、醤油などの発酵調味料の発達により、漬物はよりいっそう多様化します。

**時代と共に
多様化する漬物**

　16世紀、江戸時代に入ると漬物にする野菜の種類も増え、漬け方も単に貯蔵を目的とするのではなく、風味を大切にするようになり、当座漬け、一夜漬けなどの浅漬けの漬物が好まれるようになります。漬物のことを「おしんこ」と呼ぶことがありますが、これはもとは浅漬けを古漬けと区別する呼び名だったのです。

　晩秋から初冬にかけては、沢庵や白菜の漬物を漬け込む季節です。**都会**ではあまり見かけられなくなりまし

or other preservatives.

By the 12th century Kamakura period, pickles had been greatly refined and they were an integral part of *shōjin ryōri*, the vegetarian cuisine especially associated with Zen temples and other Buddhist establishments.

Takuan, one of Japan's most popular varieties of pickles, consisting of dried *daikon* radish pickled in salt and rice bran, is said to have been devised by a famous Zen priest named Takuan Oshō.

Somewhat later, *miso*, *sake*, *mirin* or sweet *sake* and soy sauce, all became popular as fermenting agents, which led to increasing diversity among the types of pickles available.

From the sixteenth century, and into the Edo period (1600–1868), the varieties of vegetables used to make pickles proliferated rapidly, and the motive for making pickles was no longer limited to food preservation. Flavor was now the thing, and lightly fermented pickles made from fresh vegetables preserved with salt and malt, varieties that were only salted for a short time or even overnight, became increasingly popular. Pickled vegetables are now popularly referred to collectively as *oshinko*, but originally this term was used to differentiate the newer lightly salted types from the older types.

The season for making *takuan* and pickling Chinese cabbage (*hakusai*) and other varieties of vegetables is from late autumn to early winter. In **urban areas** it's a

たが、地方の農村などでは、家族で冬中食べる漬物を大きな**樽**に漬け込むのが、今でも大切な**冬支度**の一つとなっています。

　日本ひとくち歳時記、今日は「漬物」についてお話ししました。

sight seen less often nowadays, but out in the Japanese countryside, for example in rural communities, you still find families making pickles in large **barrels** for their own consumption during the long winter months, and packing these barrels remains one of the important **preparations for winter**.

This has been *Around the Year in Japan*. On today's program we discussed *tsukemono*, or Japanese "pickles."

漬物
野菜などを塩・みそ・ぬか・こうじ・酒かす・酢などにつけた食品の総称。つけこむ期間により浅漬け、古漬けなど。香の物。おしんこ。pickles。

温　泉
Hot Springs

日本ひとくち歳時記、今日は「温泉」について
お話ししましょう。

This is *Around the Year in Japan*. Today we are
going to talk about the Japanese love for *onsen*,
or "hot springs."

日本人は今も昔も大の温泉好き

2、3日暇ができたらどうしますか、とたずねられたら、皆さんはどんな答えをするでしょうか。こんなとき、多くの日本人は、温泉にでも行ってのんびりしたい、と答えます。

日本は世界でも有数の**火山国**、したがって全国到る所に温泉が噴き出しています。ですから、観光地に行くといえば、温泉に行くのとほとんど**同義語**といってもいいくらいです。

旅行代理店のカウンターは、温泉地のパンフレットでいっぱいですし、書店の旅行関連の書棚の多くも温泉ガイドで埋められています。

テレビでも毎週のように「穴場温泉巡り」「秘湯の旅」などといった長時間番組が放送されています。

If we had two or three days free, and somebody asked us how you would like to spend them, what would we reply? Many Japanese would immediately reply that they would head for a hot springs resort to relax.

Japan is one of the world's most **volcanic countries**, and for that reason, there are many hot springs all over the country. When you say you're taking a trip in Japan, this is usually pretty much **synonymous** with going to stay at a hot springs resort.

At just about any **travel agency** counter there will be loads of pamphlets singing the praises of the waters of various hot springs resorts, and in bookstores in the travel section one can final shelf after shelf of guides to hot springs.

Nearly every week on television sees one or more lengthy programs with titles like "Tours of Little-Known Hot Springs" and "Trips to Hidden Waters" that allow

温泉地に長期滞在していた昔のお百姓さん

日本は昔から米作りを中心にした農業国でしたから、農作業は秋にいったん終わり、来年の春まで一休みというサイクルがありました。

半年以上の**重労働**に疲れた体を休めるために、あるいは痛めた体を治すために、お百姓さんたちは食料はもちろん、**炊事道具**持参で温泉に出かけました。そしてゆっくりと湯に浸かって時間を過ごしたのです。

温泉の湯には場所によって、ミネラル、**イオウ**、ラジウム、塩分などさまざまな物質が地中から溶け出しており、それが**神経痛**、**リューマチ**、胃腸病などさまざまな**病気**を治す効能を持っています。

長期滞在が前提で、宿泊費も安く設定されていましたから、短い人で数週間、長い人だと数ヵ月も温泉にとどまって体を休め、春からの農作業に臨んだのでした。

2次、3次産業従事者が大半となり、忙しくなった現在では、こんなぜいたくな過ごし方ができるのは、引退

viewers to share the delights of the waters.

Since Japan was from ancient times an agricultural nation primarily dependent on rice cultivation, most farm work came to an end with the harvest in autumn. Once the rice grain had been brought in, farmers were generally able to relax until the following spring.

After more than six months of **back-breaking labor**, they were usually weary and wracked by aches and pains, and one way of reviving themselves would be to go off to a hot springs resort, taking **cooking utensils** with them, and spend time their relaxing in the waters.

Depending on the hot spring's location, the waters contain different minerals—**sulfur**, radium, salts or other chemicals—all with different beneficial effects. Certain hot springs became famous for treating **neuralgia**, **rheumatism**, diseases of the stomach and intestines and many other **ailments**.

Because guests tended to stay at one hot spring for a long period of time, inn rates were kept cheap. A relatively short stay would be for a few weeks, while a long one might last several months. After resting up, the farmers would head back home to begin their farm work in the spring.

Nowadays most Japanese are engaged in manufacturing or service occupations, and are busy all the year round, so generally the only people who can enjoy the luxury of

したお年寄りぐらいのもので、働き盛りの人は週末の1、2泊がせいぜいといったところです。

日本全国で開発されている温泉地は2000余り、源泉数は2万を数えます。群馬県の草津、静岡県の伊豆、神奈川県の箱根、大分県の別府など、有名な温泉地の名前をあげれば切りがありません。

日本の温泉は飲むのではなく浸かるもの

泉温は40度から60度のものが大部分で、中には90度以上という温泉もあり、卵を茹でられるほどです。

国によっては、温泉は**飲用する**のが中心という所もあるようですが、日本では広い湯舟にはった湯に浸かるのが中心です。浴室にはさまざまな**趣向**が凝らされています。

香り高いヒノキで作った桧風呂、ごつごつした岩で浴室そのものを作った岩風呂、最近では浴槽の底から泡になった空気が噴き出し、体に心地よい刺激を与えてくれる泡風呂なども人気です。

でも何といっても、温泉の醍醐味は露天風呂にあるといえるでしょう。

lengthy stays at hot springs are retired old folk. Those who are working mostly have to make do with a stay or one or two nights over a weekend to take the waters.

There are more than 2,000 developed hot spring areas throughout Japan, while natural wellsprings number well over 20,000. Famous resorts are too many to mention here, although some of the best known undoubtedly are Kusatsu in Gunma Prefecture, the Izu Peninsula region in Shizuoka Prefecture, Hakone in Kanagawa Prefecture and Beppu in Ōita Prefecture.

Water temperatures usually range from 40 to 60 degrees centigrade, though some are hotter than 90 degrees —hot enough to boil an egg.

In some countries, people seem to go to hot springs resorts primarily for the purpose of **imbibing** the waters, but in Japan bathing is the prime attraction—soaking oneself in a spacious tub or pool. Quite a lot of **ingenuity** can be seen in the styles of baths and bathing areas, which vary considerably.

There are *hinoki* cypress tubs, made of cypress wood, in which the bathers can enjoy the fragrance of the wood as they soak, and *iwa buro* tubs, made out of rough rocks and boulders. Recently *awaburo* have become popular—tubs in which jets of air blow in from the bottom of the tub providing pleasant stimulation on various parts of the body.

But without a doubt, the "king" of the *onsen* is the *roten buro*, the open-air bath.

**温泉で気分を
リフレッシュさせる**

　趣のある自然をそのまま活かして作られた湯舟の湯に**浸かる**。首から下は湯で温まり、顔を心地よい**涼風**がなでて行く。上を見れば青い空。聞こえるのは湧き出る湯が流れ込む音と、周りの林を**吹き抜ける**風の音だけ。日常の生活とはまったく切り放された空間です。日ごろの仕事のことなどすっかり忘れて、リフレッシュされるのです。

　日本ひとくち歳時記、今日は「温泉」についてお話ししました。

The idea is for bathers to **soak** in pools built outside, making the most of natural features in the environment. As the bathers soak in the hot water, their faces are caressed by a refreshingly **cool breeze**. Looking up, they see blue sky. The only sound is the trickle of hot water into the bath, and the breeze **wafting** through the thickets nearby. It's possible here to feel entirely cut off from the grind of daily life. The bathers forget their daily cares, and refresh their spirits.

This has been *Around the Year in Japan*. On today's program we discussed *onsen*, or "hot springs."

温泉
1: その土地の年平均気温より高い温度の湧水 (ゆうすい)。日本の温泉法では、湧出口での温度が25℃以上か特定成分を規定量以上含むものをさす。浴用や飲用に利用される。いでゆ。hot spring。
対義:冷泉。2: 1を利用する施設のあるところ。温泉場。

冬 Winter

Part 4

鍋　物
Hot Pot Dishes

日本ひとくち歳時記、今日は「鍋物」について
お話ししましょう。

This is *Around the Year in Japan*. Today we are
going to talk about *nabemono*, or Japanese
"hot pot dishes."

**日本の冬の最大の
ごちそうは鍋料理**

冬の寒い日には暖まる料理が何よ
りのごちそう、そんな時にはど
この家庭でも「今晩は鍋にしようか」
ということになります。

　材料はじつにさまざまで、魚貝類、
肉、野菜、キノコ類、豆腐など何で
も使え、栄養もバランスがとれて豊
富です。鍋の名は、地域や材料によ
ってつけられることが多いようです。
サケを使った北海道の石狩鍋、**カキ**
を使った広島のカキ鍋など、郷土色
のある食材を使った鍋料理が日本各
地にあります。

　卓上にガスこんろなどの熱源を用
意し、大きな土鍋に水かだし汁を入

On really cold days in winter, the best type of meal is one that warms us up. On bone-chilling cold afternoons in Japan, when people start to think about what to have for their evening meal, somebody is very likely to say, "Let's have *nabe* for dinner!"

Nabe, or *nabemono*, is the collective term for various kinds of hot pots. They use a wide variety of **ingredients**, all chosen for a healthy nutritional balance, including seafood of various sorts, meat, vegetables, various mushrooms, *tōfu* or "bean curd" and all kinds of other good things. The specific names for the *nabemono* are derived from the ingredients and the region of their origin. *Nabe* include, for example, the *Ishikarinabe* of Hokkaidō, which features **salmon**, the *kakinabe* of Hiroshima, which features fresh **oysters**, and so on. *Nabe* cuisine thus varies according to the foods available from region to region.

This is how a typical *nabe* is made. A gas burner, or other type of heating source, is placed on a table, and on

れ、材料を洗って、切って、盛りつけておきさえすれば、あとは食卓でそのまま料理するだけです。主婦にとってそれほど手がかかりません。

材料がそろっていさえすれば、人数が多少増減してもかまわないことも、鍋物の良いところです。

鍋を囲むのは家族だけではありません。これからの季節、年末の忘年会や新年になってからの新年会などの折、職場の同僚や気のあった仲間で鍋料理を楽しむこともよくあります。

そんな時、張り切って鍋の番を引き受け、**だし汁の味加減**からそれぞれの食材の食べごろにまで気を配り、いっさいを取り仕切る人のことを「鍋奉行」と呼んだりします。

さまざまな種類がある鍋料理

鍋料理にはいくつかのタイプがあります。味を付けないだし汁の中に材料を入れて煮込み、ポン酢などに紅葉おろしや刻んだ**あさつき**などを加えたつけ汁につけて食べるのがその一つです。

top of this goes a large earthen pot, or *donabe*, filled either with water or light **broth** (*dashi*). The ingredients are cooked in the water or broth, so once they've been prepared—washed, cut up, and attractively arranged—that's it. Since everything is eaten right there at the table, cooking doesn't require too much effort for the housewife.

An additional advantage of cooking dinner like this is that it makes little difference how many people are eating, or when they come to the table, as long as there are enough ingredients to go around.

Families aren't the only people who enjoy a meal around the hot pot. In the cold weather months to come, especially during the year-end parties and the festivities to get the new year off to a good start, colleagues and friends will often gather around a hot pot in an eating establishment for a convivial communal meal.

At such times, one person in the group usually volunteers to be the *nabe bugyō*, or "hot pot superintendent," and takes charge of such things as **adjustment of the taste of the broth** and the particular selection and timing of ingredients to be added.

There are several different styles of *nabe*. Some hot pots are made by cooking the ingredients in an unseasoned broth and then dipping them into a sauce made with soy sauce and citrus juice, supplemented by grated radish with red chili pepper, chopped **chives** and other ingredients.

このタイプの代表的な鍋は、水炊き（メインの食材は骨付きの鶏肉です）、しゃぶしゃぶ（ごく薄く切った牛肉を沸騰した湯の中で軽く洗うようにして食べます）、フグやタイ、タラなどのちり鍋などです。

寄せ鍋はどのように作る？

もう一つのタイプは、味付けしただし汁に材料を入れて煮込み、材料から出た旨みの利いた煮汁といっしょに具を食べるタイプの鍋です。このタイプの代表的な鍋、寄せ鍋を例にとって作り方をご紹介しましょう。

材料は名前のとおり、魚貝類、肉類、エビやカニなどに、白菜、春菊、ねぎ、人参、椎茸、しめじなど好みの野菜を何でも寄せ集めて取り揃えます。だし汁が煮立ったところに、火の通りにくい材料から順番に入れて煮込みます。食べ終わって残っただし汁に、ご飯やうどんを入れて一煮立ちさせて食べるのも、おつなものです。

すき焼きは日本を代表する料理

もう一つのタイプの鍋が「すき焼き」です。底が厚く、平たい鉄製のすき焼き鍋を使い、醤油と砂糖の味の利いた濃い煮汁で、牛肉と野菜類、それにしらたき、焼き豆腐などを煮

Typical *nabe* in this style include the *mizutaki* hot pot, whose main ingredient is chicken still on the bone; *shabu shabu*, in which beef sliced paper-thin is dipped for an instant into vigorously boiling water; and *chirinabe*, a pot of vegetables and fish, typically *fugu* **blowfish**, **sea bream** or **codfish**.

In another style of hot pot the ingredients are added to a broth that has been thoroughly seasoned. The added ingredients then release additional flavors into the broth as they stew. One especially popular type in this style is *yosenabe*, meaning "mixed hot pot." Here is a typical example of *yosenabe*, to show how *nabemono* are cooked.

As the name suggests, a wide variety of ingredients are used, including fish, shellfish, meat, **shrimp**, **crab**, other seafoods, Chinese cabbage, a slightly bitter green vegetable called *shungiku*, long *negi* onions, carrots, *shiitake* and *shimeji* mushrooms, and other delicious vegetables. When the broth is ready, the ingredients are added one by one, with those that take the longest to cook going in first. After the diners have eaten all the morsels of food, it is a good idea to add rice or *udon* noodles to the remaining broth and cook it up to finish off the meal.

Another variety is *sukiyaki*, which has become quite well known. To make it, a special iron *sukiyaki* pan is used, with an extra thick, flat bottom. The cook starts with a broth made with soy sauce and sugar, into which he or she places beef, various kinds of vegetables, *shirataki* noodles,

込み、具だけ鍋から取り出し、そのまま、あるいは**溶いた生卵**をつけて食べます。

すき焼きは明治以後の食べ物

「すき焼き」というとよく代表的な日本料理の一つにあげられますが、明治時代以前の日本では、動物の肉をあまり食べませんでしたから、比較的新しい料理なのです。

もともと、鍋で煮た料理を器に移さず、直接取り出して食べることは、江戸時代までは上流社会では行われず、庶民の間だけの食べ方だったといいます。

今、鍋料理が家庭でも、営業用にも大流行なのは、それだけ食卓の民主主義が進んだ結果なのかもしれません。

日本ひとくち歳時記、今日は「鍋物」についてお話ししました。

boiled *tōfu*, and other ingredients. When the food is cooked, the diners take what they fancy with their chopsticks, and either eat it as it is or dip it into a small dish of **beaten raw egg**.

Sukiyaki is a dish that is often taken to be typically Japanese, but it is in fact a relatively recent addition to Japanese cuisine. It only became popular after the Meiji period (1868–1912). Prior to the opening to the West in the late 19th century, Japanese rarely ate meat.

One feature of *nabemono* cooking is that everybody picks out what he or she wants to eat directly from the pot. This communal style of eating around a pot was associated only with common folk and farmers up until the Edo period (1600–1868). Nobody from the upper classes would eat this way.

Nowadays, eating *nabe*-style is enjoyed both at home and in restaurants. *Nabe*-style cuisine thus offers a fine example of the democratization of eating habits in Japan.

This has been *Around the Year in Japan*. On today's program we discussed *nabemono*, or Japanese "hot pot dishes."

日本酒
Sake

日本ひとくち歳時記、今日は「日本酒」について
お話ししましょう。

This is *Around the Year in Japan*. Today we are
going to talk about *sake*.

**日本人とは切っても
切れない日本酒**

次第に夜風が冷たくなるころ、日本では、会社帰りに「熱燗で一杯」という誘惑に駆られる向きも多いようです。同僚や友人と、肴をつまみながら酒をくみ交わし、1日の疲れを癒そうというわけです。日本で飲まれるアルコールは、ビール、ウィスキー、日本酒、焼酎、ワインなどさまざまですが、寒い季節には日本酒の人気がぐっと高くなるようです。

日本酒は蒸した米に米の**こうじ**と水を加えて**発酵**させ、こして造ります。稲作と共に日本に伝来したといわれ、長い長い歴史を持っていますから、日本酒に対する日本人の愛着には並々ならぬものがあります。**辛口**、**甘口**、こくのあるもの、さらっとした味わい

As the winter nights get colder, it becomes more and more tempting for Japanese workers to stop off at a local bar on their way home and enjoy a cup of hot *sake*, or *atsukan*. Sharing a drink with one's colleagues or friends and eating small tasty side-dishes is apparently the only way to drive away the fatigue of a hard day's work. Various kinds of alcoholic drinks are available in drinking establishments in Japan, including beer, whiskey, *sake*, *shōchū* (a particular type of distilled spirits), and wine. But in winter the overwhelmingly preferred drink is *sake*, or *Nihonshu*.

Sake is **brewed** from rice, water and **yeast**. It has an extremely long history, being an integral part of the rice culture that came to Japan many centuries ago, so it is a drink for which the Japanese have an uncommon fondness and attachment. Each variety of *sake*—**dry** or **sweet**, heavy or light—has its own distinct flavor, so distinct that for some travellers having the opportunity to sample

のものなどそれぞれに特色があり、地酒を味わうのを旅行の楽しみとしている人もあるくらいです。

ではここで、日本酒の一般的な飲み方をご紹介しましょう。会社帰りのサラリーマンが2人連れだって居酒屋の暖簾をくぐったとしましょう。まず酒の注文です。好みの銘柄の酒を選び、冷やして飲むか温めて飲むかを選択します。温める温度は46度から60度までとされていて、注文するときに「熱燗で」とか「ぬるめに」とか指定します。

「とっくり」と呼ばれる陶器などの瓶に入れた酒が運ばれてくると、「ちょこ」と呼ばれるごく小さな茶碗に注いで飲みます。その際は、まずお互いに、相手のちょこに注ぎあって、相手が飲み干したらすかさず注ぎたします。

こうしてさしつさされつ、肴をつまみながら、仕事の愚痴や上司の悪口、スポーツ選手の評定から社会時評まで、気の置けないおしゃべりを楽しんだ後、最後にご飯やそばなどを食べて締めくくる……というのが、典型的なコースです。もちろん、居酒屋で飲むよりは、家でゆっくり晩酌す

日本人の典型的な日本酒の飲み方は?

exotic types of local *sake* offers the greatest thrill of the trip.

Let me give you a description of a common way in which *sake* is enjoyed. Two coworkers, on their way home from work, will stop off a local bar, going in under the traditional *noren* shop curtain, and sit down at a table. They then decide on the variety of *sake* they want to drink, and whether to drink it hot or cold. Heated *sake* is served at temperatures ranging from 46 to 60 degrees centigrade. If a person likes his *sake* hot, he will ask for *atsukan*, but if he wants it warm but not hot, he will ask for *nurume*.

The waiter or waitress will bring the *sake* in a **china flask**, known as a *tokkuri*, and it is poured from this into small cups, or *choko*. It is considered proper etiquette when two people are drinking together for each to pour for the other. Each waits for the other to drain his or her cup, and then refills it.

The two drink to each other's health, savor whatever food they have ordered, relax, and give themselves over to complaining and criticizing the hard work they do and their **bosses**, discuss sports stars, and deliver judgements on various topics in the news. Often they will finish up the session by ordering a serving of rice or noodles. Such is the standard way of enjoying a drink in a bar. Some people, however, prefer to go straight home and enjoy a

**意外に少ない
日本酒の消費量**

る方が良いという人もあります。

　統計によりますと、日本で消費されるアルコール飲料のうち、70パーセントを占めるのはビールで、日本酒はその5分の1にも及びません。別の調査では毎日ビールを飲む人が全体の24パーセントだったのに対し、日本酒を毎日飲む人は4パーセントに過ぎませんでした。これは、ビールの場合は、食前に軽く一杯、という場合や、食事中に水代わりに飲んだり、スポーツ観戦中に飲んだり、色々な飲み方をするのに加え、日本酒を飲む人のうちでも、まず**アルコール度数の低い**ビールから始めて、日本酒へ移るという飲み方をする人が少なくないなどの事情があるためと思われます。

　しかし、**若い世代**では、日本酒よりはワイン、ビール、ウィスキーなどの洋酒を好む人が増えつつあるのは否定できない情勢で、日本酒業界では、若い女性をターゲットにした軽い**甘口の酒**を開発するなどの努力を続けています。

　日本ひとくち歳時記、今日は「日本酒」についてお話ししました。

drink over dinner, instead of stopping off on the way.

Statistics show that 70 percent of the alcohol consumed in Japan is beer, while *sake* accounts for less than 20 percent. Another survey shows that while 24 percent of respondents drink beer on a daily basis, a mere 4 percent drink *sake* daily. The reasons for this lie in the variety of occasions on which beer is drunk: some people enjoy a glass before meals, or they may drink beer instead of water during their meal, and they also enjoy beer while watching sports at stadiums. Furthermore, many *sake* drinkers start off their drinking sessions with a glass or two of beer because of its relatively **low alcohol content**.

It is an undeniable fact that among the **younger generation** a growing number of individuals prefer wine, beer, whisky or other Western beverages to *sake*. *Sake* brewers have consequently been trying their best to come up with new varieties of **sweet-flavored** *sake* with, for example, a special appeal to young women.

This has been *Around the Year in Japan*. On today's program we discussed *sake*.

こたつ
Kotatsu

日本ひとくち歳時記、今日は「こたつ」について
お話ししましょう。

This is *Around the Year in Japan*. Today we are
going to talk about *kotatsu*, or leg warmers.

**日本の家屋の造りは
夏涼しく冬寒い**

14 世紀の歌人で有名な随筆集を
残している吉田兼好は、「家
の作りようは夏をむねとすべし」とい
う有名な言葉を残しています。冬の寒
さは暖房の工夫でどうにかできるが、
日本の夏は蒸し暑く、耐えがたい。
だから家の内外を風が吹き抜けるよう
にし、なるべく涼しく暮らせるように
すべきだという趣旨です。

　なるほど、伝統的な日本家屋の構
造は、**屋根**や壁は薄くして熱がこも
らないようにし、床は地面から数十
センチ上に荒く板を敷き、その上に
藺草を編んで作った畳が敷いてあり
ます。窓は大きく作られ、床から**天井**
の高さまで開いている部屋も多くあ
りますし、部屋と部屋の間仕切りも
壁ではなく、木の枠に丈夫な紙を貼

The 14th-century poet Yoshida Kenkō left a famous essay in which he gave the advice that if you want to build a house you should do it with summer comfort in mind. His point was that in winter it is possible to combat the cold with various heating appliances and clothes, but the humid weather of summer is much more difficult to deal with unless you have a house that is airy and cool.

This is true, and in the past Japanese houses were constructed accordingly, with relatively thin **roofs** and walls, so that summer heat would not remain trapped inside, and floors several dozen centimeters above the ground, their rough planking covered with straw *tatami* mats. Often windows would be large, and the space between **ceiling** and floor kept free and open. Rooms would be divided not by walls but by sliding doors constructed of papered wooden frames which could be

った襖でできていて、取り払うことができるようになっています。つまり、外の涼しい風がつねに部屋の中を通り抜けるようになっているのです。

　冷房などというものがなかった時代には、夏の暑さをどうしのぐかが、家造りでは第一の関心事だったのです。でも冬はどうなるのでしょうか。特にシベリアからの強い寒気が吹き込む日本海側は、世界でもっとも積雪が多い地方の一つといわれているのです。

　何しろ、家の中を風が吹き抜けるように造ってあるのですから、暖炉などで家中を暖かく保つことはまったく不可能でした。そこで、家の中のある部屋に**暖房設備**を作り、家族みんながそこに集まって、家族団らんをするという形が生まれたのです。

**昔のこたつの作りは
今とはだいぶ違う**

　その一つが今日お話しする「こたつ」です。今では**都会**ではなかなか見られなくなりましたが、30〜40年ほど前まで多くの家にあったものは、こんな作りになっていました。

　部屋の真ん中に、90センチ四方、ちょうど、畳半分の大きさに床が掘り下げられ、その中心部が炉になっていて、中で**炭**が燃やせるようになってい

removed when desired. In other words, during the sti-
fling summer months, everything possible was done to
keep cool breezes circulating through the rooms.

In the days before such things as fans and air condi-
tioners were available, the primary concern was to build
homes in a way that would lessen the summer heat. But
how were things in wintertime? In winter the Japan Sea
side of Honshū is one of the areas of highest snowfall in
the world, and it gets the freezing winds that blow in
from Siberia.

It was, of course, quite impossible to heat a Japanese
house, built to allow a free flow of air, in its entirety by,
say, a centrally located fireplace. So what people did was
to build a **heating device** in certain rooms of the house,
and here the family would gather together, keep warm,
and enjoy the closeness of family life.

The *kotatsu* started out as one of these heating
devices. Although nowadays the original types of *kotatsu*
have become a rare sight in houses in **urban areas**, up
until 30 or 40 years ago they were to be seen in many
homes.

Traditional *kotatsu* consisted of a pit in the center of
the floor of a room, about 90 centimeters square (the
size of half a *tatami* mat). In the center of the pit would
be placed a stove, inside which **charcoal** would be

ます。炭は山の木をいったん蒸し焼きにして作ってありますから、火をつけてもまったく煙が出ません。そして長時間適度の強さで安定して燃えます。

この炉の上に、ちょうどこの穴の部分を覆うように高さ40センチほどのやぐらを置き、大きな布団をかけます。そしてこの穴の周囲に座って足を入れ、暖まるのです。これがこたつです。

火の上に布団をかけてしまうのですから、何だか聞いただけでは、今にも火事になってしまいそうですが、大丈夫。寒い外から帰宅して、このこたつの中に足を入れると、ホッと一息つく感じがします。こたつにつきものなのが、この時期に出回るみかんです。こたつの上のカゴに山盛りにされたみかんを食べながら、家族の会話が弾むというのが日本の冬の風物詩でした。

変わってきた最近の日本の暖房事情

しかし、最近ではだいぶ様子が変わってきました。暖房の中心が、石油やガスを使ったストーブに代わったのです。また「日本の家屋は夏をむねとすべし」でもなくなってきたのも変化の理由の一つです。というのも、エアコンが普及してどの家庭でも冷

burned. Charcoal, made by charring timber, was smoke-free and gave off a good deal of heat for a long period of time.

Over the stove was a tablelike structure about 40 centimeters high, on top of which would be a coverlet. Everybody sat around the stove with their legs dangling into the pit, covered by the coverlet.

A coverlet? What about the risk of fire, you might say. In fact, the *kotatsu* was quite safe. When people came into the house out of the cold, they would slip their legs in under the coverlet and breathe a sigh of relief at the warmth. Usually there would also be a large pile of mandarin oranges placed on the table to munch on while discussing the events of the day. This was a typical family scene in winter.

Things have changed greatly in recent decades as far as the *kotatsu* is concerned. In most cases people now rely primarily on oil or gas for their heating needs. Also the style of the Japanese home has changed—it's no longer summer oriented. Air-conditioning units are now widely used, and most family homes have one. This has effected the design and structure of Japanese houses.

房が使えるようになり、家の造りも外の風を遮断し、密閉できる構造の家が増えてきたことがあげられます。

　ですから、最近ではストーブからさらに、暖かい風を送り込む温風ヒーター、床から暖める床暖房などに代わってきています。こたつにもぐり込んでじっとしているなどという過ごし方ではなく、暖かく暖房された部屋の中で自由に動き回る生活様式になったのです。

**現在でも依然として
根強いこたつ人気**

　でも、こたつは少し姿を変えて、今でも根強い人気を保っています。やぐらの天井部分に電気で熱するヒーターを取り付け、布団をかける「電気ごたつ」です。これなら、簡単に移動できますし、不要な時にはしまっておくこともできます。

　こたつの中でぬくぬくとしながら、みかんを食べ、本を読み、ゆっくりと過ごす。日本の冬ならではの過ごし方でしょう。

　日本ひとくち歳時記、今日は「こたつ」についてお話ししました。

More and more houses are now designed to be fairly airtight, preventing the movement of air from inside to out and vise versa.

Recently many people have changed from stoves to the much warmer fan heaters, which circulate warm air, and to floorboards heated from underneath. This is a reflection of the change in people's lifestyles in the home: instead of sitting for hours on end around the *kotatsu*, they can now move around freely from heated room to heated room.

Kotatsu have changed somewhat from what they used to be, but they still remain popular with some Japanese. They are now electric, with electric heaters installed inside their tablelike structure, and a coverlet spread over the top. They can be moved freely from room to room, and put in storage when no longer needed.

Sitting in a *kotatsu*, eating mandarin oranges and reading one's favorite book, is a particular pleasure enjoyed in winter, and one probably enjoyed only in Japan.

This has been *Around the Year in Japan*. On today's program we discusssed *kotatsu*, or leg warmers.

風　邪
Colds

日本ひとくち歳時記、今日は「風邪の民間療法」について
お話ししましょう。

This is *Around the Year in Japan*. Today we are
going to talk about colds and traditional cold
remedies.

風邪はだれもがかかる
ありふれた病気

朝起きてみたら、何だか鼻水が出
る。くしゃみが続けて3回出た。
咳も出る。喉がいがらっぽい……。こ
のような症状が出たら「あっ、風邪だ」
と思いますね。冬の初めのこの時期、
日本では特に風邪をひく人が多いよう
に思われます。風邪はもっともありふ
れた病気で、たいていの人は年に2、
3度はかかるのではないでしょうか。

　風邪をひいたなと思っても高熱が
出ない限り、すぐに医者に行くとい
う人は少なく、市販の風邪薬を飲む
とか、風邪に効くといわれる民間療
法を一つ二つやって様子を見るとい
う人が多いようです。事実そんな程
度で3、4日で治ってしまう場合も少
なくないからです。

　日本で風邪の民間療法として古く

We get up in the morning and realize we have the **snuffles**. We sneeze three times in a row. And then cough. Our throat feels somehow rough and sore.... With these **symptoms**, the first thing we're likely to think is, "Uh-oh, I've got a cold!" At this time of year, the start of winter, people seem to catch cold right, left and center in Japan. Indeed, the common cold is indeed a very common complaint, probably afflicting the average person two or three times a year.

Few people go immediately to the doctor once they've decided they've caught a cold, unless they show signs of a raging fever. Usually, they head straight for the pharmacy to buy a commercial **cold medicine** over the counter. Quite a few individuals will try a folk remedy or two. And quite often, these measures are enough to send their cold on its way in three or four days.

We'd like to tell you about a few of the traditional

風邪の民間療法とは
どのようなものか?

から伝えられているものをいくつかご紹介しましょう。

まず、多くの人があげるのが卵酒です。日本酒を熱くした中に生卵を入れて、よくかき混ぜて飲むというものです。好みで砂糖や蜂蜜を入れて甘くします。

次にあげられるのが**ショウガ**です。すりおろしてお湯を注いで飲むことが多いようです。砂糖を入れて甘くしたり、しょうゆや味噌で味付けすることもあります。刻んだネギを入れた味噌汁も効くようです。この場合のネギはタマネギではなく日本ネギです。梅の実を干して塩漬けにした梅干しも風邪に効くといわれています。

また、ネギや**ニンニク**は薄く切って喉に張ると**喉の痛み**が取れるといわれます。喉の痛みには、**きんかん**という香りの良いちいさな柑橘類の実を砂糖漬けにしたものを食べるとか、大根を蜂蜜に漬けておいて、出てきた汁を飲む、**蓮根**（ハスの根っこ）をおろして絞った汁を飲む、なども効果があるといわれています。

folk remedies for colds used in Japan since time immemorial.

One remedy many people swear by is *tamagozake*, or Japanese egg nogg. You break a raw egg into heated *sake*, stir well, and then drink it. Some people like to sweeten the concoction with sugar or honey.

Another thing that apparently works wonders is raw **ginger** in one form or another. Many people are apparently quite fond of a concoction that is an infusion of ginger and hot water. Some like it sweetened with sugar, or else flavored with soy sauce or *miso* bean paste. Yet another effective remedy is a simple broth made of ordinary bean paste to which slices of long onion have been added. The Japanese onion used in this case, known as *negi*, is not the usual kind of onion but a long green type similar to the Welsh onion. *Umeboshi*, or apricots pickled in sea salt, are another favorite cold cure.

Some people believe *negi* onions or **garlic** sliced thinly and applied to the throat are the best cure for a **sore throat**. Other popular cures for a sore throat include eating tiny, flavorsome sugar-coated **kumquats**, drinking the juice that seeps out of *daikon* radishes when they are steeped in honey, and drinking the juice of grated **lotus roots**.

**世界中にある
風邪の民間療法**

いかがでしょうか。皆さんがお住まいの所にも、似たような療法が伝えられているのではないでしょうか。世界各地で風邪の民間療法として伝えられていることを調べてみると、かなり共通の部分があるそうです。その多くは体を温めたり、発汗を促すような刺激的な匂いや味があったり、水分を**補給する**などの働きがあるものです。

そもそも風邪の原因の80パーセント以上は**ウィルス**で、しかもウィルス自体にはほとんど効く薬もないため、風邪薬として売られている薬は症状を和らげる効果しかないといわれています。長い間人々が試してきた民間療法を行って、後は安静にしているというのは十分に効果的なやり方なのです。

もっとも、日本には「風邪は万病のもと」という言葉もあるように、風邪をこじらせると**肺炎**など重大な病気になることもありますから、1週間たっても症状がとれない時には医者に行った方が良いようです。

日本ひとくち歳時記、今日は「風邪の民間療法」についてお話ししました。

The countries of our listeners probably have folk remedies quite similar to the ones we have been describing. Folk remedies for colds as they have come down to us through the years share many common characteristics throughout the world. That is to say, most of them involve ingredients with a strong smell or taste and have the effect of warming up the body and making the sufferer sweat, as well as **replenishing** the body's supply of fluids, and so on.

Over 80 percent of colds are said to be caused by **viruses**, and since very few medicines have any real effect on them, commercial cold remedies really only alleviate or mask the symptoms until the body can recover on its own. The best way to combat a cold is to use some of these old time-tested folk remedies, and give the body ample rest.

There is a saying in Japan: "Colds are the origin of countless diseases." That is say, if a cold gets worse, it can develop into something far more serious, such as **pneumonia**. So if cold symptoms don't go away after a week or so of using these traditional cold remedies, you should pay a visit to the doctor.

This has been *Around the Year in Japan*. On today's program we discussed colds and traditional cold remedies.

雪
Snow

日本ひとくち歳時記、今日は「雪」について
お話ししましょう。

This is *Around the Year in Japan*. Today we are
going to talk about snow.

**日本は世界でも
有数の降雪地帯**

日本が世界でも有数の降雪地帯を抱える国だということは案外知られていません。東北から南西へと連なる島々からなる日本は、ほとんどの地域が**温帯**に属していて、とびきり寒い国というわけではありませんが、冬の**季節風**が大量の降雪をもたらすのです。12月から3月にかけて、日本各地の**スキー場**は若者たちでいっぱい。もう少し年輩の人々の間では、温泉に浸かり、雪見酒を楽しむという人も少なくありません。

　日本でもっとも雪の多い地方は、最北に位置する北海道ではなく、本州の北西部分です。これは、遠くシベリアから吹いてくる冷たい季節風が、暖流の流れる日本海の上を渡って来る時に大量の水分を含み、本州

Many people don't realize that Japan is one of the snowiest countries in the world. The Japanese archipelago stretches in a long arc from northeast to southwest, for the most part in the **temperate zone**, so as a whole the Japanese climate is not as cold as many other countries farther north. Nevertheless, during winter, the **seasonal winds** do bring substantial snowfall. From December to March, the **ski slopes** are crowded with young people, and older people take the waters at *onsen*, or hot springs resorts, perhaps enjoying a cup of *sake* while taking in the snow scenes.

Surprisingly enough, the area of greatest snowfall in Japan is not its northernmost region, namely the island of Hokkaidō, but the northwestern region of the main island of Honshū. Here cold seasonal winds blow in from Siberia, **slamming right into the mountains** that run down the spine of the main Japanese island. These cold winds

の中央部分を走る**山脈に突き当たって**雪を降らせるからです。

日本海側に降雪が集中する理由

ですから冬の間、本州の西側、つまり日本海側は雪が多く、多い所では年間100日も降雪があるのに対して、本州の東側つまり太平洋側はよく晴れて乾燥する所が多いのです。

ノーベル文学賞を受賞した日本の作家、川端康成の代表作『雪国』の冒頭の一節が「国境の長いトンネルを抜けると、雪国であった」となっているのは、山脈の両側で**ガラリと気候の変わる**日本の風土の特徴をよく表現しています。

本州の太平洋側にある首都東京などでは、年に数日しか雪が降らないことが多いため、雪が降ると子供たちは大喜びで**雪だるま**を作ったり**雪合戦**をしたりして楽しみます。しかし、日常的に雪に対する備えをしていませんから、**交通事故**が多発したり電車が遅れたり、雪の量は少なくても案外大きな影響をもたらします。

一方積雪の多い地方では、日常生活で被（こうむ）る影響はさらに大きなものがあります。2メートル、3メートルも

have passed over the relatively warm waters of the Japan Sea on their way and they hold substantial amounts of moisture, which is what causes the snow to fall so heavily.

This is why in winter snowfall is heavy on the Japan Sea side of Honshū, but much less on the Pacific side. On the western side of the archipelago some areas experience as many as 100 days of snowfall, while on the Pacific side the weather is most often clear and dry.

Nobel Literature Laureate Kawabata Yasunari put it well in a famous passage in his novel *Yukiguni* (*Snow Country*): "The train emerged from the long tunnel that ran through the border, and suddenly they were in snow country." Kawabata skillfully evokes the **abrupt change of weather** from Japan's Pacific side to the Japan Sea side, a distinctive feature of Japan's climate.

Cities and towns around Tōkyō on the Pacific side of Honshū may have only a few days of snowfall per year, so when the white stuff falls, children have great fun, building **snowmen** and having **snowball fights**. But since these parts of the country are not accustomed to heavy snowfall, residents tend to be ill prepared, and many **traffic accidents** occur and trains are delayed. Even a relatively light snowfall can have an unexpectedly large impact.

Of course, in areas where snowfall is heavy, the impact is even greater. In localities which regularly experience snow piling up to two or three meters, there is

の積雪になる地方では、雪の重みで家がつぶれるおそれがあるため、時々屋根の上に登って雪下ろしをしなければなりません。これは大変な**重労働**であるうえに、雪下ろしの途中で屋根から落ちてけがをする人もいます。また、病院や学校に通うのもままならないなど、雪国に住む人々の苦労は外からでははかり知れないものがあります。

雪国で行うさまざまな雪対策とは?

こうした中、雪国の人々は雪に対処するためにさまざまな工夫を凝らしてきました。豪雪地帯の家は、急勾配の屋根を持ち、建物の2階部分にも出入り口をつけた独特の造りをしています。庭の樹木には、てっぺんから円錐形に綱を張り巡らせて、**枝が**折れるのを防ぎます。

また、雪を利用して貯蔵庫を作り、天然の大きな冷蔵庫として食物の貯蔵に用いるなど、積極的な雪の利用も行っています。

さらに、**雪の彫刻**の展示会を開いたり、雪になじみの薄い地域の人々のために、雪を体験するツアーを企画し、ちゃっかり雪下ろしの手伝いをさせてしまうなど、アイデアを凝ら

the risk that houses might collapse due to the heavy weight of the snow, and every now and then people have to go up on their roofs to clear them off. Besides being a **back-breaking job**, this can also be dangerous, since people may be injured in falls. People living in snow country sometimes encounter tremendous problems trying to get to hospitals and schools. Even the simple tasks of daily life are affected in ways that people living in areas of the country with little snowfall find difficult to imagine.

Consequently, people who live in snowy parts of Japan have come up with many ingenious ideas for dealing with the snow. Homes in areas of heavy snowfall often have steep sloped roofs, and they are often designed to allow access from the second floor if the snow has cut off access to the first floor. Trees in gardens are wrapped in supportive **straw ropes** to prevent their **limbs** from breaking under the weight of snow.

It's very common for residents of snow country to take advantage of the elements and build "iceboxes" in the snow to preserve food.

Another thing people in these snowy areas do is hold exhibitions of **snow sculptures**. Local governments in snow country have been trying all sorts of other ideas to get people to come and experience the snow. There are tours, for example, so that people from localities

す地方都市も見られます。

　日本ひとくち歳時記、今日は「雪」についてお話ししました。

with scant snow can experience for themselves what it is like to live in the snow country—taking a hand in clearing snow, and so on.

This has been *Around the Year in Japan*. On today's program we discussed snow.

雪
1: 寒いときに空から降ってくる白くつめたいもの。水が氷の結晶になって降るもの。水蒸気を多量に含んだ空気が上昇冷却し、昇華して結晶となる。六角形の結晶が基本で、針状や角柱状および板状結晶など多様な形がある。snow。**用例** 一が積もる。一が降る。2: 白くて美しいものの形容。snowy。**用例** 一の肌。3: しらが。gray hair。4: 紋所の名。雪の結晶を紋章化したもの。
雪と墨（ゆきとすみ）正反対に違うことのたとえ。
雪に白鷺（ゆきにしらさぎ）見分けにくいこと。また、目立たないことのたとえ。**類似** 闇夜に烏（からす）。
雪に閉ざされる（ゆきにとざされる）雪のために外部との連絡がとれなくなる。be snowbound。
雪は豊年の兆し（ゆきはほうねんのきざし）大雪が降るのは、豊作になる前ぶれであるという言いつたえ。
雪を欺く（ゆきをあざむく）非常に白いさまをいう。
雪を戴く（ゆきをいただく）1: 山の頂上に雪が積もる。snow-capped　2: 白髪で、頭が真っ白になる。gray-haired。
雪を回らす（ゆきをめぐらす）風に舞う雪のように、美しく舞う。

年賀状
New Year's Greeting Cards

日本ひとくち歳時記、今日は「年賀状」について
お話ししましょう。

This is *Around the Year in Japan*. Today we are
going to talk about *nengajō*, or "New Year's greeting cards."

1月1日は初日の出、おせち料理で始まる

1月1日の朝。日本で一番静かなひとときです。大晦日の夜遅くまで寝ずに年越しの行事をして、ゆっくりと起きる家族もあれば、朝早く起きて初日の出を拝んでから、少しうとうととまどろむ人もいます。

いつもより遅めの時間に家族が1年最初の食卓を囲み、薬草を漬け込んだお酒、お屠蘇を飲み、揃ってお正月の料理であるお雑煮やおせち料理に箸をつけ、ゆっくりと過ごします。普段は忙しく行き交う人で一杯の通りも、この時ばかりは人通りもまばら、清々しい風が吹きわたるようです。

そんな中、郵便配達の人たちだけは忙しく街を走ります。年賀状の配達です。一つの家庭ごとに、小包ほどの大きさの束になった年賀状がど

It's New Year's morning in Japan, one of the quietest days of the entire year. While some families get up in a leisurely manner, after staying up late the previous night to observe New Year's events, others may be up earlier than usual to see in the dawn—or they may now be taking a short nap.

The first breakfast of the year is much later than usual, and special dishes, *o-sechi ryōri*, await family members when they sit down for a leisurely meal. *Sake* in which herbs and spices have been steeped, and *o-zōni*, a New Year's soup with ricecakes, are among the delicious treats. Outside, the streets, normally busy with people, are quite empty, with only cold winds sweeping along them.

Some people are extremely busy at this time of year— the postal service workers. They're delivering *nengajō*, or New Year's greeting cards. In Japan, the tradition is for New Year's greeting cards to start being delivered on the

っさりと届けられますと、さっそく、家族一人一人に仕分けられ、おせち料理もそこそこに読みふけります。

○○さんは今年も元気そうだ、△▽ちゃんはもうこんな歳になったのね、などと書いてくれた人の近況が披露されます。日本人にとって、年賀状はお正月の大きな楽しみといえるでしょう。

人それぞれの年賀状の工夫の凝らし方

年賀状の趣向はさまざまです。すべて毛筆の手書きで出す人、毎年の干支（えと）にちなんだ絵などを自分でデザインして出す人、文面を指定して印刷屋に頼む人、家族の写真をそのままはがきにして出す人、などなど。

年賀状用に簡単な写真製版ができる機械も、年末近くになると文具店、デパートなどの店頭に並びます。もちろん最近ではパソコンで文字、写真などをレイアウトし、印刷所顔負けの立派な出来栄えのものを送る人も増えてきました。

パソコン用のカラープリンターの価

very first day of the New Year. Every family receives a stack of New Year's postcards bundled together, and they're passed out among the members to read while enjoying New Year's *o-sechi ryōri*.

The snippets of news written on the *nengajō* let you get an idea of how their senders are doing. Ah, Mr. and Mrs. So and So are well again this year. Goodness, is their daughter really that big already? Reading the greeting cards that come from friends, relations and colleagues is one of the enjoyable pleasures of the New Year for most Japanese.

There are all sorts of *nengajō*. Some people like to make their own by hand, writing the messages with a brush and designing motifs with that year's particular animal from the **Chinese zodiac**. Others ask printers' shops, which do a thriving business at this time of year, to make up *nengajō* according to various specifications. Many people like to have a photograph of all the family on the greeting cards they print.

Toward the year's end, all sorts of devices to print *nengajō* with photographs can be found at **stationery shops** and department stores. Of course, an increasing number of people now send cards produced on personal computers, with lettering and printing fine enough to match any print-shop's.

This year, now that color printers for personal com-

格がぐっと下がって、一般の人の手に届くようになってきたことから、今年あたりは、例年よりずっとカラフルで斬新なデザインの年賀状が交換されることになりそうです。

日本人は1人何枚ぐらいの年賀状を出すのでしょうか。

年齢や職業によってまちまちです。小学生ぐらいですと、おじいちゃん、おばあちゃん、ごく親しい友だちなどせいぜい10枚ぐらいでしょうか。

これが年齢が上になるにつれて枚数も増え、社会人となって仕事上のつき合いが増えると100枚を超えるのは当たり前、働き盛りの人になると200枚、300枚というのもまれではありません。中には1人で1000枚、2000枚と膨大な数の年賀状を出す人もいます。

郵政省が1997年10月31日に発売した年賀はがきは41億7680万枚。これは赤ちゃんを含めた国民1人当たりにすると、35枚ということになりますから、日本人がいかに多くの年賀状を出すかが分かるでしょう。今年売れた41億7680万枚のはがきのうち2億枚が、パソコンのプリンターできれいに印刷できる特殊な紙を使って発売

日本人はどれくらいの年賀状を出すのか?

puters have fallen in price, it looks as if the average person will be able to make and send *nengajō* that are even more brilliantly colorful than ever.

On the average, how many New Year's cards, do you think one person sends out each year?

The answer to this depends on age and occupation. A primary school student might send a dozen or so—to grandparents and close friends.

Usually, the older the person, the more cards he or she sends. When people start jobs and careers, they often send more than 100 cards to colleagues and associates, and it's not uncommon to send 200 or even 300. Some people send huge numbers—one or even two thousand.

Consider this statistic: on October 31, 1997, the **Ministry of Posts and Telecommunications** put on sale an amazing 4,176,800,000 New Year's greeting cards. In terms of the total population of Japan, including babies, this means that each person sent 35 New Year's cards. Starting this year, the Ministry of Posts and Telecommunications put on sale a special type of card for PC printers. Of the 4 billion odd New Year's cards sold, 200 million were of this type. This will give you an idea of how attached

されました。

賞品が楽しみなお年玉つき年賀はがき

さて、いま話に出たお年玉つき年賀はがきとはいったい何でしょうか。

はがきの表の下の部分に番号がプリントしてあります。そして1月15日に行われる抽選で、1等から4等までの賞品が当たるというのが、このお年玉つき年賀はがきなのです。

今年の1等は、テレビ、ビデオカメラなど。4等はお年玉切手シート。これがなかなか人気があって、上の順位の賞品よりこちらの方が欲しいという人もいるくらいです。

日本の郵便制度では、はがきの表に年賀状であることを明記して、12月25日ぐらいまでにポストに入れれば、必ず1月1日に配達してくれるようになっています。

この制度が定められたのは1899年で、もう100年近い歴史を持っていますが、1949年に郵政省がお年玉つき年賀はがきの発売を始めたところ、これが爆発的な人気を呼び、年賀郵便は年ごとに増え、年賀状の交換がすっかり国民の間に定着したのです。

年末から年始にかけての郵便局は、目の回るような忙しさ。毎年、高校

Japanese are to their New Year's greeting cards.

What exactly do New Year's lottery greeting cards look like?

They're basically like any other postcard, but at the bottom of each one there's a lottery number. On January 15, a national lottery is held using these cards, with prizes in four categories.

The first category this year includes TVs, video cameras and similar goods. The fourth category are sheets of commemorative stamps—and very popular they are, with some people preferring these to the more valuable prizes.

The Post Office guarantees delivery on New Year's day of all greeting cards posted by December 25.

This is a system that was instituted nearly a century ago—1899 to be exact—and it has functioned with incredible efficiency ever since. The system of New Year's lottery postcards, however, only began in 1949. It led to a huge boom in the sales of greeting cards. The number of cards sent out by people increased year by year. The New Year's *nengajō* lottery is now a fixed institution.

This is why Japan's post offices are incredibly busy places at the end and the beginning of each year. Every

生、大学生など大勢のアルバイトを
動員して、年賀状の整理や配達など
の対応に追われます。郵便局の人た
ちがお正月休みをゆっくりと楽しめる
のは、他の人たちが休みから明けた
後です。

　日本ひとくち歳時記、今日は「年
賀状」についてお話ししました。

year all kinds of young people—mainly high school and university students—are mobilized on a temporary basis to sort and deliver the huge piles of cards. The workers in the post offices in Japan are only able to take it easy once everybody else's New Year is over.

This has been *Around the Year in Japan*. On today's program we discussed *nengajō*, or "New Year's greeting cards."

年賀状
年始の祝賀状。年賀状を書く風習は平安時代からあるが、今日の年賀郵便の形態は、明治初期に郵便はがきが発行されてからのもの。New Year's card。

成人式
Coming-of-Age Ceremonies

日本ひとくち歳時記、今日は「成人式」について
お話ししましょう。

This is *Around the Year in Japan*. Today we are
going to talk about *seijin-shiki*, or "Coming-of-Age
Ceremonies."

**成人式は1948年に
祝日として制定**

1月15日、正月の行事も終わり、
日常のリズムを取り戻したころの
この日、街では再び晴れ着を着た女
性の姿があちこちで見られます。

1月15日は、**国民の祝日**の一つで
ある「成人の日」です。1948年に、
20歳になった青年たちを祝う日とし
て制定され、全国のあちこちで「成
人式」が行われます。今日は、この
成人式についてご紹介しましょう。

日本では20歳になると法的に成人
としての**権利と義務**を持つものとさ
れ、選挙権が与えられ、飲酒や喫煙
の自由も認められます。1998年の1
月15日現在で満20歳の青年の数は**総
務庁**の推計で174万人。このところ
毎年数万人ずつ減り続けています。

Don't forget these candies!

It is January 15. The numerous events and celebrations to mark the New Year have already been wound up, and daily life has returned to its normal pace. But on this day in Japan you once again see lots young women walking through the town decked out in beautiful kimono.

The reason is that January 15 is Coming-of-Age Day, and a **national holiday**. It was established as a special holiday in 1948 for young people of both sexes who have turned 20. On this day, special coming-of-age ceremonies are held throughout Japan. Here is how Japanese people celebrate this day.

In Japan, when a person turns 20, he or she becomes a full-fledged citizen, legally endowed with the **rights and responsibilities** of an adult—and also allowed legally to vote, smoke and drink. On January 15, 1998, the **Management and Coordination Agency** estimates that around 1,740,000 Japanese had turned 20 in the previous year. Recently the number of new adults has

成人式の起源は
古くにさかのぼる

一人前の大人として認められる通過儀礼としての「成人式」の起源は非常に古いもののようで、その形式や、成年式を受ける年齢は、時代や身分、地方、また男女によって多種多様です。

公の記録としては、714年に**皇太子**が「元服」を行ったというのがもっとも古いものです。これはいわば**貴族社会**の「成人式」で、内容は、髪型を変え、冠をかぶり、大人の服装に変え、また名を変えるなどというものでした。

農民などの間では、どれだけ一人前の仕事ができるようになったかを田植えや草刈りなどで試すことなどがよく見られました。また、重い石を担いだり、徹夜で正座したりできたものを成人と認める地方もあったといいます。

現在では20歳になれば自動的に成人とされるため、昔のように通過儀礼としては重んじられなくなりましたが、1月15日には市町村など**地方自治体**の多くが「成人式」を行っています。女性たちは、この日のために、

been declining by tens of thousands each year.

The Coming-of-Age Ceremony has its origin in rituals and ceremonies that used to be held in ancient times to confirm that a person had indeed become an adult. The forms these ceremonies took, however, and the age at which they were held, have varied greatly depending on the era, the social status of the youngster, the region and the sex.

The oldest official record of such a ceremony, the *genpuku* ceremony carried out for the **Crown Prince**, dates back to 714. This ritual was a kind of coming-of-age ceremony performed within **aristocratic society**. Among other things, it involved a change in hair style and the donning of an official cap and adult robes for the first time, as well as the adoption of a new adult name.

Among the farming population, however, it was often the case that a person had to demonstrate that he had reached adulthood by performing particular tasks, such as planting the rice fields and cutting grass. In some regions young men were required to perform tests of endurance, such as carrying heavy stones or sitting in an upright formal position throughout the night.

Nowadays, young people simply have to reach the age of 20 to be considered adult, so the traditional rites are no longer followed. Nevertheless, on January 15, most **local governments** sponsor Coming-of-Age Ceremonies for the new adults in their districts. Young ladies have gorgeous new long-sleeved kimono specially

かなり高額な振り袖を新調したり、貸衣裳屋から借りたりして、装いもとても華やかです。

時代につれて 様変わりする成人式

式典では自治体の長や来賓の祝辞、若者の側からの成人を迎えての**決意表明**などのスピーチが行われますが、近ごろでは、あまり堅苦しい内容だと若者が集まらないというので、ポップ・コンサートやカラオケ大会を開くなど工夫を凝らす所が増えています。

それでも、スピーチの最中に私語が多いとか、会場に入らずにロビーでおしゃべりばかりしているものが少なくないなど、主催者である大人たちをあきれさせる光景が目につくということです。

しかし、一方で、NHKが毎年この日に行っている、若者たちによるスピーチ大会「青春メッセージ」では、若者たちが熱のこもったスピーチを行い、大人たちの感動を呼んでいます。

日本ひとくち歳時記、今日は「成人式」についてお話ししました。

made, or rent them from kimono shops just for that day.

At the ceremony, there will be speeches from the local mayor or other senior officials and specially invited guests, and representatives of the young people will read **pledges of their determination** to act as responsible adults. Recently, aware that the stiffness and formality of the ceremonies tends to put most young people off, sponsors have been staging pop music concerts, *karaoke* jamborees and other events intended to attract the young.

Even so, there are apparently sights that scandalize the sponsers—young people chattering away right through the addresses, or people not even bothering to come into the hall for the official ceremonies, but simply remaining outside in the lobby to gossip.

On the other hand, each year on Coming-of-Age Day, NHK holds a large speech contest for young people, under the title "Messages from Youth." The speeches are very compelling and often move older listeners deeply.

This has been *Around the Year in Japan*. On today's program we discussed *seijin-shiki*, or "Coming-of-Age Ceremonies."

節　分
Setsubun

日本ひとくち歳時記、今日は「節分」について
お話ししましょう。

This is *Around the Year in Japan*. Today we
are going to talk about *Setsubun*, or "Bean
Throwing Day."

**節分とは季節の
変わり目のこと**

日本の自然の特徴の一つは、四季がはっきりしていることだといわれます。この四季の分かれ目の日を「節分」と呼びます。ですから本来は春、夏、秋、冬それぞれの季節の変わり目にあるのですが、現在は冬から春への変わり目、立春の前日だけを特別に「節分」と呼び、全国各地の神社や仏閣で、また家庭でも、**節分行事**をします。

1998年は2月4日が立春ですから2月3日が節分に当たりますが、この日に節分豆（煎った**大豆**）を「鬼は外、福は内」と大声で唱えながらまきます。

豆をまくのは年男（その年の干支

No-rio

One of the distinctive features of Japan's weather is said to be that there are clear differences between the four seasons. The term *setsubun* was originally used to refer to the turning point from one season to the next. There were consequently four such turning points, marking the changes between spring, summer, autumn and winter. Nowadays, however, *Setsubun* is used specifically to refer to the day before the first day of spring (known as *Risshun*). On this day **Setsubun rites** are carried out at Shinto shrines and Buddhist temples throughout Japan, as well as in private homes.

In 1998, the first day of spring was February 4, so *Setsubun* fell on the previous day, February 3. The ceremony of *Setsubun* consists of scattering **roasted soybeans** and shouting, "*Fuku wa uchi, oni wa soto!*" which literally means, "In with good fortune, demons get out!" The idea is to invite good fortune in, and to drive away bad luck.

The people who scatter the beans in public cere-

に当たる男性）の役とされますが、家庭では普通、家の主人が務めます。

節分にまつわる
さまざまな風習とは?

また、柊（ひいらぎ）の枝に焼いた**イワシ**の頭を刺して、垣根や門塀の上にかかげておく風習もあります。こうしておくと**鬼**や**疫病神**が柊の刺をいやがり、イワシの悪臭を嫌って逃げて行くと考えたようです。地方によっては**ニンニク**やネギなどを入口に吊り下げておく所もあるようです。

豆まきのあと、自分の年齢と同じ数だけ豆を拾って食べると病気にかからない、という言い伝えもあります。節分豆を食べて一年の無病息災を祈り、春の訪れを喜ぶのです。

農村では囲炉裏に12粒の豆を並べ、その焼け具合で一年の各月の天候や、農作物の出来を占う「豆占（まめうら）」をする風習もありました。

ところで、節分に豆をまく習わしは、中国では紀元前の周の時代にすでにあった、という記録が残っていますが、それが日本に伝わり広まった

monies are usually *toshi otoko*, or men whose birth animal by the Chinese zodiac is the one for that particular year. In homes, it's usually the head of the household who takes on the role.

Another practice associated with *Setsubun* was to hoist the head of a roasted **sardine** on a stick of **holly** and hang it on top of the fence or front entrance. **Demons** and various **gods of pestilence** were traditionally believed to hate the holly and find the smell of the sardine repugnant, and quickly make their escape. In some regions, **garlic**, leeks or other strong-smelling plants such as onions were hung up with the same purpose.

After the ceremony of scattering roasted soybeans, it's the custom to eat some—as many as the number of years we have lived. This practice is said to ward off illness. Thus, one celebrates the coming of spring by praying for safety from diseases and illness.

In farming communities there was also a tradition of "bean divination": 12 beans would be lined up in the *irori*, or sunken family hearth, and the patterns formed by the heat on the beans as they roasted would offer hints on what the weather would be like in particular months and thus what kind of harvests could be looked forward to.

Records show that a practice of scattering soybeans already existed in Zhou Dynasty China. This is the practice that entered Japan. Until the Kamakura period, around the middle of the 13th Century, it was called

ようです。鎌倉時代の末ごろ（13世紀半ば）までは「追儺」、あるいは「鬼遣」と呼び、赤鬼、青鬼に扮した人に豆を投げつけて悪疫を追い払う、朝廷の行事として大晦日に行われていました。

現在の節分は江戸時代に定着

それが現在のように立春の前日の行事として定着したのは14世紀、室町時代になってから、さらに一般庶民の間に広がったのは町人文化が花開いた17世紀、江戸時代に入ってからのことでした。

今も豆まきをしている家庭がどのくらいあるのか、正確には分かりませんが、節分の日には各地の有名な神社やお寺で、大相撲の力士や歌舞伎役者、人気歌手などを年男として招き、豆まきをする様子がテレビや新聞で必ず報道されます。

節分が近づくと、スーパーや菓子屋の店先に節分豆が鬼のお面といっしょに売られているのも目につきますから、案外多くの家庭で豆まきの情景が見られるのかもしれません。

日本ひとくち歳時記、今日は「節分」についてお話ししました。

tsuina, meaning "driving out calamity," and *oniyarai*, meaning "driving out the demons." In these ceremonies, held on New Year's Eve at the Imperial Court, officials threw beans at men dressed up as red devils and blue devils in order to drive out misfortune and calamity.

The present rite for dispelling evil influences on the day before the arrival of spring took root in the 14th Century, during the Muromachi period. It spread to ordinary folk during the 17th Century in the Edo period, a time when the townsmen's culture flourished.

It's not clear how many Japanese families still engage in the ceremony of scattering beans. But many famous shrines and temples invite *sumō* wrestlers, *kabuki* actors, popular male singers and other public personalities to do the bean throwing at their ceremonies, and these are always given wide coverage on TV, in the newspapers and other media.

As *Setsubun* nears, we start to notice supermarkets and confectionery shops with stands selling roasted soybeans, together with the appropriate demon masks. So it's possible that quite a few families still engage in the traditional bean-throwing rite.

This has been *Around the Year in Japan*. On today's program we discussed *Setsubun*, or "Bean Throwing Day."

NHK「日本ひとくち歳時記」 執筆者

春
ひな祭り	水戸
卒業式	島村
花 見	水戸
こいのぼり	佐久間
花粉症	島村
駅 弁	佐久間
ワサビ	佐久間
日本茶	佐久間

夏
カツオ	水戸
梅 雨	水戸
梅干し	佐久間
ボーナス	島村
七 夕	水戸
おばけ	水戸
盆踊り	佐久間
浴 衣	島村

秋
地 震	水戸
台 風	佐久間
運動会	島村
米	水戸
紅葉狩り	島村
七五三	佐久間
漬 物	島村
温 泉	佐久間

冬
鍋 物	島村
日本酒	水戸
こたつ	佐久間
風 邪	水戸
雪	水戸
年賀状	佐久間
成人式	水戸
節 分	島村

佐久間 実 (さくま みのる)
1948年、神奈川県生まれ。東京外国語大学ドイツ科卒業。1971年NHK入局。アナウンサー、報道局ディレクターなどを経て、現在、国際放送局ドイツ語放送担当。

島村 美穂子 (しまむら みほこ)
1946年、北海道生まれ。津田塾大学学芸部卒業。1969年NHK入局。家庭番組、生涯学習、国際放送局ロシア語放送担当を経て、現在、NHKエデュケーショナル放送大学業務室。

水戸 晴子 (みと はるこ)
1948年、東京生まれ。慶応大学文学部卒業。1971年NHK入局。生涯教育、語学番組ディレクターを経て、現在、国際放送局朝鮮語放送担当。

本書はNHKの国際放送「NHKワールド・ラジオ日本」で放送された台本をもとに出版したものです。

　NHKの国際放送「NHKワールド」は、テレビとラジオを通して世界に情報を発信し、日本への理解を進めるとともに、海外にいる日本人に最新の情報を届けています。

　テレビ国際放送「NHKワールドTV」は、1998年10月以降、世界のほぼ全域に放送され、NHKのニュース・情報番組が、リアルタイムでどこでも視聴できます。

　ラジオ国際放送「ラジオ日本」は、全世界に向けて1日のべ65時間、短波により、日本語と英語を含む22の言語で放送しています。短波ラジオと周波数の表を準備すれば、世界中どこでも「ラジオ日本」を良好に聴くことができます。

　「NHKワールド」は、もともと海外向けの放送のため、日本国内はサービスの対象には含まれていませんが、日本国内からも、ホームページを通じて様々な情報を楽しむことができます。

　ラジオの周波数表などは、下記に申し込むことができます。（日本国内の方は返信用の90円切手の同封が必要です。なお日本語放送の周波数表などは、ファックス・サービスでも入手できます。海外からもアクセス可能で、24時間対応です。）

「NHKワールド」問い合わせ先

〒150-8001　NHK国際放送局国際編成部「NHKワールド」係

Tel　03-3465-1111（代表）平日午前10時〜午後7時

Fax　03-3481-1350

E-mail　worldtv@intl.nhk.or.jp（NHKワールドTV）

　　　　info@intl.nhk.or.jp（ラジオ日本）

ファックス・サービス　03-5454-0888（ラジオ日本の日本語放送＝情報番号260を入力し、スタートボタンを押す。）（NHKワールドTV番組表＝情報番号258を入力し、スタートボタンを押す。）

Internet Home Page

　http://www.nhk.or.jp/nhkworld/（NHKワールドTV）

　http://www.nhk.or.jp/rjnet/（ラジオ日本）

NHK「日本ひとくち歳時記」
Around the Year in Japan

1998年7月31日　第1刷発行

編　者　NHK国際放送局「日本一口事典」プロジェクト
　　　　講談社インターナショナル株式会社

発行者　野間佐和子

発行所　講談社インターナショナル 株式会社
　　　　〒112-8652　東京都文京区音羽1-17-14
　　　　電話：03-3944-6493（編集）
　　　　　　　03-3944-6492（営業）

印刷所　大日本印刷 株式会社

製本所　株式会社 堅省堂

英語で話す「日本」Q&A
Talking About Japan Q & A

KBB 1

講談社インターナショナル 編　　　　　320ページ　ISBN 4-7700-2026-0

外国の人と話すとき、必ず出てくる話題は「日本」のこと。でも英語力よりも前に困るのは、日本について知らないことがいっぱいという事実です。モヤモヤの知識をスッキリさせてくれる「日本再発見」の書。

英語で話す「アメリカ」Q&A
Talking About the USA Q & A

KBB 21

賀川 洋 著　　　　　304ページ　ISBN 4-7700-2005-8

仕事でも留学でも遊びでも、アメリカ人と交際するとき、知っておくと役に立つ「アメリカ小事典」。アメリカ人の精神と社会システムにポイントをおいた解説により、自然、歴史、政治、文化、そして人をバイリンガルで紹介します。

英語で話す「世界」Q&A
Talking About the World Q & A

KBB 19

講談社インターナショナル 編　　　　　320ページ　ISBN 4-7700-2006-6

今、世界にはいくつの国家があるか、ご存じですか? 対立をはらみながらも、急速に1つの運命共同体になっていく「世界」——外国の人と話すとき知らなければならない「世界」に関する国際人必携の「常識集」です。

英語で読む日本史
Japanese History : 11 Experts Reflect on the Past

KBB 4

英文日本大事典 編 　　　　　　　　　　224ページ　ISBN 4-7700-2024-4

11人の超一流ジャパノロジストたちが英語で書き下ろした日本全史。外国人の目から見た日本史はどういうものか、また日本の歴史事項を英語で何と表現するのか。新しい視点が想像力をかき立てます。

日本を創った100人
100 Japanese You Should Know

KBB 25

板坂 元 監修　英文日本大事典 編 　　　　　240ページ　ISBN4-7700-2159-3

混乱と激動を乗り越え築き上げられた現在の日本。その長い歴史の節目節目で大きな役割を果たした歴史上のキーパーソン100人を、超一流のジャパノロジストたちが解説。グローバルな大競争時代を迎えた今、彼らの生き方が大きな指針となります。

英語で話す「日本の謎」Q&A 　外国人が聞きたがる100のWHY
100 Tough Questions for Japan

KBB 11

板坂 元 監修 　　　　　　　　　　　　　240ページ　ISBN 4-7700-2091-0

なぜ、結婚式は教会で、葬式はお寺でなんてことができるの？　なぜ、大人までがマンガを読むの？　なぜ、時間とお金をかけてお茶を飲む練習をするの？──こんな外国人の問いをつきつめてゆくと、日本文化の核心が見えてきます。

英語で話す「日本の心」 　和英辞典では引けないキーワード197
Keys to the Japanese Heart and Soul

KBB 12

英文日本大事典 編 　　　　　　　　　　328ページ　ISBN 4-7700-2082-1

一流のジャパノロジスト53人が解説した「日本の心」を知るためのキーワード集。「わび」「さび」「義理人情」「甘え」「根回し」「談合」「みそぎ」など、日本人特有の「心の動き」を外国人に説明するための強力なツールです。

英語で話す「日本の文化」
Japan as I See It

KBB 22

NHK国際放送局文化プロジェクト 編　ダン・ケニー 訳　196ページ　ISBN 4-7700-2197-6

金田一春彦、遠藤周作、梅原猛、平川祐弘、西堀栄三郎、鯖村豊之、野村万作、井上靖、小松左京、中根千枝の１０人が、日本文化の「謎」を解く。NHKの国際放送で２１の言語で放送され、分かりやすいと世界中で大好評。

茶の本
The Book of Tea

KBB 28

岡倉天心 著　千 宗室 序と跋　浅野 晃 訳　264ページ　ISBN 4-7700-2379-0

一碗の茶をすする、そのささやかで簡潔な行為の中に、偉大な精神が宿っている──茶道によせて、日本と東洋の精神文化の素晴らしさを明かし、アジアの理想が回復されることを英文で呼びかけた本書は、日本の心を英語で明かす不朽の名著。

武士道
BUSHIDO

KBB 30

新渡戸稲造 著　須知徳平 訳　　　　　312ページ　ISBN 4-7700-2402-9

「日本が生んだ最大の国際人」新渡戸博士が英語で著した世界的名著。「日本の精神文化を知る最良の書」として世界17ヵ国語に翻訳され、1世紀にわたって読みつがれてきた不滅の日本人論。国際人必読の1冊。

ニッポン不思議発見！　日本文化を英語で語る50の名エッセイ集
Discover Japan: Words, Customs and Concepts

KBB 14

日本文化研究所 編　松本道弘 訳　　　　　260ページ　ISBN 4-7700-2142-9

絶望的な場合ですら、日本人は「そこをなんとか」という言葉を使って、相手に甘えようとする……こんな指摘をうけると、いかに日本人は独特なものの考え方をしているか分かります。あなたも「不思議」を発見してみませんか。

ニッポン見聞録　大好きな日本人に贈る新・開国論
Heisei Highs and Lows

KBB 8

トム・リード 著　　　　　216ページ　ISBN 4-7700-2092-9

国際化の進む日本ですが、アメリカのジャーナリストが鋭い目と耳で浮き彫りにしたニッポンの姿は、驚くほど平穏でいとおしく、恥ずかしいくらい強欲で無知なものでした。トムが大好きな日本人へ贈る新・開国論。

「Japan」クリッピング　ワシントンポストが書いた「日本」
Views of Japan from The Washington Post Newsroom

KBB 6

東郷茂彦 著　　　　　256ページ　ISBN 4-7700-2023-6

アメリカの世論をリードするワシントン・ポストに書かれた「Japan」……政治、外交、経済、社会のジャンルで取り上げられた日本の姿を、国際ジャーナリストが解説し、その背後にある問題点を浮き彫りにする一冊。

NHK「ニュースのキーワード」
NHK: Key Words in the News

KBB 26

NHK国際放送局　「ニュースのキーワード」プロジェクト 編　232ページ　ISBN4-7700-2342-1

日本で話題になっている時事問題を解説する、NHK国際放送の番組「ニュースのキーワード」から「総会屋」「日本版ビッグバン」「ダイオキシン」など、33のキーワードを収録しました。国際的観点からの解説が、現代の日本の姿を浮き彫りにします。

ベスト・オブ・天声人語
VOX POPULI, VOX DEI

KBB 23

朝日新聞論説委員室 著　朝日イブニングニュース 訳　280ページ　ISBN4-7700-2166-6

「天声人語」は「朝日新聞」の名コラムというよりも、日本を代表するコラムです。香港返還、アムラー現象、たまごっち、マザー・テレサの死など、現代を読み解く傑作56編を、社会・世相、政治、スポーツなどのジャンル別に収録しました。

誤解される日本人　外国人がとまどう41の疑問
The Inscrutable Japanese
KBB 20

メリディアン・リソーシス・アソシエイツ 編　賀川 洋 著　　　　224ページ　ISBN 4-7700-2129-1

あなたのちょっとした仕草や表情が大きな誤解を招いているかもしれません。「日本人はどんなときに誤解を受けるのか？」そのメカニズムを解説し、「どのように外国人に説明すればよいか」最善の解決策を披露します。

ビジュアル 英語で読む日本国憲法
The Constitution of Japan
KBB 18

英文日本大百科事典 編　　　　208ページ　ISBN 4-7700-2191-7

難しいと思っていた「日本国憲法」も、英語で読むと不思議とよく分かります。日本国憲法を、59点の写真を使って、バイリンガルで分かりやすく解説しました。条文中に出てくる難解な日本語には、ルビや説明がついています。

イラスト 日本まるごと事典
Japan at a Glance
KBB 17

インターナショナル・インターンシップ・プログラムス 著　　　248ページ（2色刷）　ISBN 4-7700-2080-5

1000点以上のイラストを使って日本のすべてを紹介──自然、文化、社会はもちろんのこと、折り紙の折り方、着物の着方から、ナベで米を炊く方法や「あっちむいてホイ」の遊び方まで国際交流に必要な知識とノウハウを満載。

英語で折り紙
Origami in English
KBB 3

山口 真 著　　　　160ページ　ISBN 4-7700-2027-9

たった一枚の紙から無数の造形が生まれ出る……外国の人たちは、その面白さに目を見張ります。折るとき、英語で説明できるようにバイリンガルにしました。ホームステイ、留学、海外駐在に必携の一冊です。

英語で日本料理
100 Recipes from Japanese Cooking
KBB 15

辻調理師専門学校　畑耕一郎、近藤一樹 著
268ページ（カラー口絵16ページ）　ISBN 4-7700-2079-1

外国の人と親しくなる最高の手段は、日本料理を作ってあげること、そしてその作り方を教えてあげることです。代表的な日本料理100品の作り方を、外国の計量法も入れながら、バイリンガルで分かりやすく解説しました。

ドタンバのマナー
The Ultimate Guide to Etiquette in Japan
KBB 27

サトウサンペイ 著　　　　240ページ（オールカラー）　ISBN 4-7700-2193-3

サンペイ流家元が自らしでかした「日常のヘマ」「海外でのヘマ」を一目で分かるようにマンガにした、フレッシュマンに贈る究極のマナー集。新社会人必読！知っていればすむことなのに、知らないために嫌われたり、憎まれてはかないません。

アメリカ日常生活のマナーQ＆A
Do As Americans Do

KBB 13

ジェームス・M・バーダマン, 倫子・バーダマン 著 　　　256ページ　ISBN 4-7700-2128-3

"How do you do?" に "How do you do?" と答えてはいけないということ、ご存知でしたか？　日本では当たり前と思われていたことがマナー違反だったのです。旅行で、駐在で、留学でアメリカに行く人必携のマナー集。

日米比較 冠婚葬祭のマナー
Do It Right : Japanese & American Social Etiquette

KBB 2

ジェームス・M・バーダマン, 倫子・バーダマン 著 　　　184ページ　ISBN 4-7700-2025-2

アメリカでは結婚式や葬式はどのように行われるのか？　お祝いや香典は？……そしてアメリカの人たちも、日本の事情を知りたがります。これだけあればもう困らない。日米冠婚葬祭マニュアル、バイリンガル版。

英語で話す「仏教」Q＆A
Talking About Buddhism Q & A

KBB 24

高田佳人 著　ジェームス・M・バーダマン 訳 　　　240ページ　ISBN4-7700-2161-5

四十九日までに7回も法事をするのは、「亡くなった人が7回受ける裁判をこの世から応援するため」だということ、ご存じでしたか？　これだけは知っておきたい「仏教」に関することがらを、やさしい英語で説明できるようにした入門書です。

まんが 日本昔ばなし
Once Upon a Time in Japan

KBB 16

川内彩友美 編　ラルフ・マッカーシー 訳 　　　160ページ　ISBN 4-7700-2173-9

人気テレビシリーズ「まんが日本昔ばなし」から、「桃太郎」「金太郎」「一寸法師」など、より抜きの名作8話をラルフ・マッカーシーの名訳でお届けします。ホームステイなどでも役に立つ一冊です。

まんが 日本昔ばなし 妖しのお話
Once Upon a Time in *Ghostly* Japan

KBB 29

川内彩友美 編　ラルフ・マッカーシー 訳 　　　152ページ　ISBN 4-7700-2347-2

妖しく、怖く、心に響く昔ばなしの名作を英語で読む。人気テレビシリーズ「まんが日本昔ばなし」から、「鶴の恩返し」「雪女」「舌切り雀」「耳なし芳一」「分福茶釜」など8話を収録しました。

ベスト・オブ 宮沢賢治短編集
The Tales of Miyazawa Kenji

KBB 5

宮沢賢治 著　ジョン・ベスター 訳 　　　208ページ　ISBN 4-7700-2081-3

「注文の多い料理店」「どんぐりと山猫」「祭の晩」「鹿踊りのはじまり」「土神ときつね」「オツベルと象」「毒もみの好きな署長さん」「セロ弾きのゴーシュ」の代表作8編を精選。ジョン・ベスターの名訳でどうぞ。

銀河鉄道の夜
Night Train to the Stars

KBB 10

宮沢賢治 著　ジョン・ベスター 訳　　　　176ページ　ISBN 4-7700-2131-3

賢治童話の中でも最も人気の高い「銀河鉄道の夜」は、賢治の宗教心と科学精神が反映された独特の世界——天空、自然、大地がみごとに描かれ、光と音と動きに満ち溢れています。ジョバンニと一緒に銀河を旅してみませんか。

ベスト・オブ 窓ぎわのトットちゃん
Best of Totto-chan : The Little Girl at the Window

KBB 9

黒柳徹子 著　ドロシー・ブリトン 訳　　　　232ページ　ISBN 4-7700-2127-5

小学校一年生にして「退学」になったトットちゃんは、転校先の校長先生に「君は本当はいい子なんだよ」と温かい言葉のシャワーで励まされます……バイリンガル版で、あの空前の大ベストセラーの感動をもう一度！

マザー・グース　愛される唄70選
Mother Goose : 70 Nursery Rhymes

KBB 7

谷川俊太郎 訳　渡辺 茂 解説　　　　176ページ　ISBN 4-7700-2078-3

「マイ・フェア・レディー」や「お熱いのがお好き」という題名も、マザー・グースからの引用だったってこと、ご存じでしたか？ 英米人にとって必須教養であるこの童謡集を、詩人・谷川俊太郎の名訳と共にお楽しみください。

ビジネスマン必携！

対訳　英語で話す日本経済Q&A
A Bilingual Guide to the Japanese Economy

NHK国際放送局経済プロジェクト・
大和総研経済調査部 編

46判（128 x 188 mm）　仮製　368ページ
ISBN 4-7700-1942-4

NHK国際放送で好評を得た番組が本になりました。クイズと会話形式で楽しく読んでいくうちに、日本経済の仕組が分かり、同時に英語にも強くなっていきます。日本語と英語の対応がひと目で分かる編集上の工夫もいっぱい。

対訳 おくのほそ道
The Narrow Road to Oku

松尾芭蕉 著　ドナルド・キーン 訳
宮田雅之 切り絵
A5判変型（140 x 226 mm）
仮製 188ページ（カラー口絵41点）
ISBN 4-7700-2028-7

古典文学の最高峰のひとつ「おくのほそ道」をドナルド・キーンが新訳しました。画家、宮田雅之が精魂を込めた切り絵の魅力とあいまって、この名作に新しい生命が吹き込まれた、必読の1冊です。

対訳 竹取物語
The Tale of the Bamboo Cutter

川端康成 現代語訳
ドナルド・キーン 英訳　宮田雅之 切り絵
A5判変型・横長（226 x 148 mm）
仮製 箱入り 180ページ（カラー口絵16点）
ISBN 4-7700-2329-4

ノーベル賞作家の現代語訳と傑出した芸術家の作品、そして日本文学の研究に一生を捧げたジャパノロジストの翻訳が合体した、大人のための「竹取物語」。

英文版 ジャパン：四季と文化
Japan : The Cycle of Life

[序文] 高円宮憲仁親王殿下
[イントロダクション] C.W. ニコル
A4判変型（228 x 297 mm）
上製 296ページ（オールカラー）
ISBN 4-7700-2088-0

日本の文化は「四季」によって育まれてきました。日本人の生活、文化、精神から切り離せないこの「四季」を、美しく新鮮な数々のカラー写真でビジュアルに紹介します。

第1部　自然と風土
第2部　人々の暮らしと伝統行事
第3部　文化と伝統

英語と日本語で楽しむ

対訳 サザエさん（全12巻）

The Wonderful World of Sazae-san

長谷川町子 著　ジュールス・ヤング 訳

- 吹き出しの中にオリジナルの暖かい雰囲気を大切にした英語、
  コマの横に日本語がつく対訳形式。
- お正月、こいのぼり、忘年会など日本独特の文化や習慣には、
  欄外に英語の解説つき。

46判変型（113 x 188 mm）仮製

楽しく読んで英語が身につく
講談社英語文庫
Kodansha English Library

 特色

古典から最新話題作まで、幅広いジャンルの作品が英語で読めます。

英語の初心者から上級者まで十分読みごたえのある、さまざまなレベルの作品が揃っています。

なるべく辞書を使わずに楽しく読めるよう、原則として巻末にNotes（語句の解説）をつけてあります。

人気イラストレーターによる美しい装画、さし絵が人気です。

比較的大きめの活字を使った、読みやすい英文が好評です。

海外の作品

J・D・サリンジャー	ライ麦畑でつかまえて
	ナイン・ストーリーズ
ウイリアム・サローヤン	パパ・ユア クレイジー
エリック・シーガル	ラブ・ストーリィ
アーウィン・ショー	夏服を着た女たち
ズフェルト	星占いの本
チャールズ・ディケンズ	クリスマス・キャロル
コナン・ドイル	シャーロック・ホームズの冒険
P・L・トラヴァース	メアリー・ポピンズ
C・W・ニコル	風を見た少年
L・フランク・バーム	オズの魔法使い
ラフカディオ・ハーン	怪談
ピート・ハミル	ニューヨーク・スケッチブック
J・M・バリ	ピーター・パン
F・スコット・フィッツジェラルド	華麗なるギャツビー
アラン・ブース	マクベス*
アーネスト・ヘミングウェイ	老人と海
O・ヘンリー	O・ヘンリー短編集
カースティン・マカイヴァー	聖書ものがたり*
	聖書の名言集*
ラルフ・マッカーシー	イソップ物語*
	アラビアンナイト*
	ギリシャ神話*
	アメリカ昔ばなし*
A・A・ミルン	クマのプーさん
サマセット・モーム	モーム短編集
L・M・モンゴメリ	赤毛のアン
	続・赤毛のアン
トーベ・ヤンソン	たのしいムーミン一家
キャサリン・ルビンスタイン	ラブレターズ
ローラ・インガルス・ワイルダー	大草原の小さな家
オスカー・ワイルド	幸福な王子
(絵) 小林与志	マザーグース
	マザーグース 2
	マザーグース 3

*印は、原作をもとに英語文庫のために書き下ろした作品です